EH NA?

AN INQUIRY INTO THE RELATIONSHIP BETWEEN RATIONALITY AND MYSTICISM

By

Nick Thomas

"Take nothing on faith and apply your own intelligence"

EH NA?
AN INQUIRY INTO THE RELATIONSHIP BETWEEN RATIONALITY AND MYSTICISM

By Nick Thomas

Produced, Designed, Illustrated and Edited by
White Crane Publishing Ltd
2 Red House Square
Moulton Park
Northampton
Northamptonshire
NN3 6WL

www.whitecranepublishing.com

Text © 2012 Nick Thomas.
Additional material © 2012 White Crane Publishing Ltd.

All rights reserved. No part of this publication may be reproduced,
stored in any retrieval system or transmitted by any means,
electronic, mechanical, photocopying, or otherwise,
without the prior written permission of the
publisher and copyright holder.

British Library Cataloguing-in-Publication Data:
A CIP record for this book is available from
the British Library.

ISBN: 978-1-907347-05-4 (pbk)
First Edition.

The views of the author do not necessarily
reflect those of the publisher.

DEDICATION

Dedicated to Amy and Spencer Thomas,

for making my existence possible;

and to

Aleister Crowley, Ludwig Wittgenstein, and Eliezer Yudkowsky,

for making these thoughts possible.

CONTENTS

Acknowledgements	viii
List Of Illustrations	ix
A Note On Truth	3
Introduction	5

Part One — A Rational Analysis Of Mysticism		15
1	Mystical Experience	19
2	Logic And Experience	27
3	Rationality	37
4	Rationality And Intuitions	57
5	Archetypes	71
6	Mystical Thinking	91
7	Mystical Practices	119

Part Two — Duality And Non-Duality		127
8	Nothing	129
9	Happiness And Sorrow	143
10	Soliloquy On Free Will And The World Part One	157
11	Soliloquy On Free Will And The World Part Two	173
12	Soliloquy On Free Will And The World Part Three	183
13	Turning Back	197

Index	201

ACKNOWLEDGEMENTS

The Author wishes to express his deepest thanks to the following people and organisations for their kind permission in using their quotes:

Eliezer Yudkowsky.

Ordo Templi Orientis, for use of Aleister Crowley's quotes which are © Ordo Templi Orientis, All rights reserved.

L/L Research, for use of the Ra Material quotes which are © L/L Research, www.llresearch.org

MIT Press for use of Hao Wan's quote from *A Logical Journey: From Gödel to Philosophy.*

Every reasonable effort has been made to trace the copyright holders of the quotes used within this book, but if any have been inadvertently overlooked then the publisher would be glad to hear from them.

LIST OF ILLUSTRATIONS

Fig. 1:	An Analysis of the Concept 'Mysticism'	73
Fig. 2:	The Kabbalah Tree of Life	74
Fig. 3:	The Tarot	75
Fig. 4:	The Twelve Astrological Signs	76
Fig. 5:	The Four Elements	76
Fig. 6:	The Seven Chakras	77
Fig. 7:	The Enneagram	78
Fig. 8:	The Taijitu	79
Fig. 9:	The Symbol of Jehovih	108
Fig. 10:	The AUM	110
Fig. 11:	Table 1	163
Fig. 12:	Table 2	165
Fig. 13:	An Atom	170
Fig. 14:	Pair of Atoms	170
Fig. 15:	A Cluster of Atoms	170
Fig. 16:	A Representation of the Number Five	174
Fig. 17:	The Number Five Represented as Atoms	174
Fig. 18:	Atom Relation	179
Fig. 19:	Alternative Atom Relation 1	179
Fig. 20:	Alternative Atom Relation 2	179

EH NA?

AN INQUIRY INTO THE RELATIONSHIP BETWEEN RATIONALITY AND MYSTICISM

A NOTE ON TRUTH

This book consists of lies. In this respect it is an ordinary work of non-fiction. I am writing this book with a clear conscience for the reason that the fact that you are reading it indicates that you want me to lie to you. I also have a clear conscience because I do one better in honesty than most non-fiction authors by stating at the beginning that I am in fact lying. If you do not want to be lied to, then I recommend that you put this book down and stare at a wall.

However, I will warn you that if you think any thoughts while you are staring at that wall, you will still be being lied to, except that then you will be lying to yourself, and you are almost certainly better at lying to yourself than I would be at lying to you. (This is not meant to be an insult; we are very good at lying to ourselves.) Conversely, if you do decide to read this book, you would be correct to dismiss everything in it as a lie, but you would be deceiving yourself in doing so if your motivation for dismissing a particular lie was simply that it was not consonant with the lies you like to tell yourself. If you did take every lie herein as seriously as you take all of the lies you tell yourself, my hope is that it might help you to start lying to yourself less, though I am not certain that it will.

In this book are only lies and no truth. I have not said that we cannot find the truth; I have only said that we cannot find it in books. You may ask obligingly, "Where can we find it?" though I have just said that we cannot find it in books.

For my part, my inquiries into truth are always at the very beginning. Every step forward leaves me still at the beginning. The reason for this is that if, in stepping forward, I move past the starting line, I have ceased to inquire into truth at all, though I only come to realize this after travelling a certain distance. When I realize it, I return to the beginning. May you find many new beginnings herein!

"If for many years you practice the techniques and submit yourself to strict constraints, it may be that you will glimpse the center. Then you will see how all techniques are one technique, and you will move correctly without feeling constrained.

Musashi wrote: 'When you appreciate the power of nature, knowing the rhythm of any situation, you will be able to hit the enemy naturally and strike naturally. All this is the Way of the Void.'"

- Eliezer Yudkowsky, "The Twelve Virtues of Rationality"

INTRODUCTION

WHEN I was eighteen, I began to feel that my life had no meaning, and that it was all a great illusion which, for some reason I found myself stuck in. I passionately desired to know reality; to know something which did not have the dreamlike quality of my everyday experiences. I wished also, more than I had ever wished, for a life filled with joy, purpose and richness of experience.

This search led me to various interesting places, and eventually coalesced into something quite definite. It all happened when an odd series of events led me, in my freshman year of college, to begin studying the works of the famous occultist Aleister Crowley. Crowley claimed to have gained access to a hidden reality, and he had developed theories explaining the nature of this reality, and methods for replicating his findings. I felt that Crowley had found what I was looking for, and his skeptical, intellectual approach fit well with my own inclinations. So I began studying according to the system he had laid out.

He recommended practices of various kinds designed to induce ecstatic states of consciousness in which one would allegedly experience the reality which he had encountered. These practices were often very difficult, and I did not rise to the challenge right away.

Within a few months, however, I had reached the point that I was engaging in various physical and mental exercises for two or three hours every day. I devoted much additional time to studying the theoretical aspects of Crowley's system, as well as the theories of other authors.

When a few more months had passed, I began to experience my first major results. When I meditated, my thoughts would stop and my consciousness would be filled with overwhelming ecstasies of blazing light. I felt that I had found what I was looking for. I felt that I had encountered the reality behind the illusion, and I came to believe that the basic meaning and purpose of life was to experience this reality.

I sought out a precise theoretical formulation of the truth which I felt I had discovered. In part, this was to improve my own understanding of it, and in part, this was so that I could share it with others. I encountered fairly serious difficulties in my search. I saw that the different sources, though they agreed in much of what they said, also contradicted each other on numerous points. There was a great deal that I was confused about, with no clear way to resolve the inconsistencies. But, persistently I laboured at the task, having nothing better to do.

My sophomore year of college was emotionally and existentially difficult, and the methods I was practicing ceased to work to my satisfaction. Doubts were building up. The whole structure gave out under me when I started to read Wittgenstein. His work led me to understand why I had not been able to formulate a precise explanation of the truth I had discovered. I had not been able to explain it because it was beyond language, and could not be understood by the intellect alone. At one stroke, this resolved my confusion, and simultaneously led me to reject all of the theories that I had built up for myself up to that point.

But my hunger for truth had not diminished, and so I could not end my search. I saw that my previous efforts had not been good enough. I had not been careful enough in my thinking. I needed to take the time to build things up piece by piece, rather than formulating sweeping theories which would collapse when I discovered problems with them. I began to take inspiration from the methods of academic philosophers, with their strategy of carefully developing lines of thinking in a step-wise, rational fashion.

Progress was slow, and most lines of thinking led nowhere. I began to ask more basic questions, such as, "what exactly have I been doing all this time?" I settled on a name for what I had been doing: "mysticism". I chose this word because I felt that, of all the options, it was the one that made the smallest possible number of assumptions.

Now, let us take a break from our narrative to ask another basic question: "what is mysticism?" The term as I use it encompasses three things:

i. A particular class of experiences, or states of consciousness, which we may call "mystical experiences."
ii. A set of practices which are attempts to induce mystical experiences: meditation, prayer, etc. These we may call "mystical practices."
iii. An area of human thought, consisting of philosophical doctrines (Taoism, Vedantism, etc.) put forth by people who had mystical experiences. This we may call "mystical thinking."

Of these the most difficult to explain is mystical experience, and yet it is the crux of the whole matter. In a religious context such an experience might be described as a "vision of God." In a more scientific, psychological terminology we might call it an "ecstatic state" or a "trance state." To approach the problem of what mystical experience really is (that is, by doing more than merely throwing vocabulary at it, as I have just done), is to invite extraordinary perplexity and frustration. This we will do several times in the coming chapters; but for now we will let the problem lie.

Mystical techniques are anything done to induce mystical experiences. Such techniques include meditation, prayer, dancing, music, ingestion of drugs, various types of ritual, modification of breathing, fasting, sensory deprivation, techniques involving sexuality, and so forth. Such techniques seem to have been used in virtually every culture.

Mystical thinking encompasses a variety of doctrines that invariably accompany any practice of mysticism. They offer an interpretation for the experience, and generally also answer virtually every existentially important question, providing a comprehensive "answer to life." Such philosophies are exemplified by the Upanishads, the Tao Te Ching, the Buddha's philosophy, and also certainly by parts of the Bible.

There is a strong relationship between mysticism and religion. Each of the Abrahamic religions has its own school of mysticism. There is Christian mysticism, Jewish mysticism, and Sufism (the mystical branch of Islam). In the Eastern religions (Hinduism,

Buddhism, Taoism, etc.,) there is not such a clear division between the mainstream religion and its mystical aspect; the two are, to a greater extent, merged.

There are also schools of mysticism which are not connected with any religion. A historically important example is the mysticism of the Ancient Greek intellectuals. In modern times, nonreligious schools of mysticism include Western occultism and aspects of the New Age movement. The phenomenologists (Husserl, Heidegger, Sartre, etc.,) were, to a great extent, mystics. There was also a strain of mysticism which sprung out of the 1960s psychedelic movement, exemplified by individuals such as Timothy Leary, Aldous Huxley, and Richard Alpert.

Besides the major mystical traditions, one can find a great deal of mysticism which seems to exist outside of any tradition. I have personally met many individuals who had mystical experiences, did things to induce these experiences, and had ideas about life typical of mystics, but who were not involved in any recognizable mystical tradition. In some cases, they had hardly ever read anything on the subject. Their mysticism, it seems, had been generated wholly from inside themselves, without significant aid from cultural input. That this apparently happens, supports the hypothesis that mysticism is not merely a social construct, but a natural function of the human organism.

Similarly, if one looks, one can find works by isolated thinkers which are clearly attempting to convey mystical insights, but which again have nothing to do with any religion or major mystical tradition. Famous examples are Hegel, Schopenhauer, Wittgenstein, and Heidegger. Nietzsche also had his mystical moods.

Many great scientists and mathematicians had mystical leanings. Examples are Isaac Newton, Albert Einstein, Niels Bohr, and Kurt Gödel.

Mysticism, as we can see, is a loosely organized phenomenon. It is not a social movement, in the same way that Christianity or occultism is a social movement. Rather, it is a particular psychological state (the mystical experience), and a set of things which tend to spring up wherever this psychological state shows itself. These things include a particular flavor of thought which is unmistakably identifiable by anybody who has "been there." Since this psychological state can occur in any cultural context, people have found many different ways to express it and respond to it.

INTRODUCTION

Let us now continue with our narrative. When you left me, I was struggling to piece together an explanation of the truths which had been revealed to me as a result of my study under Aleister Crowley's system of mysticism.

At this juncture, I had mostly stopped doing the practices, due to my feeling that they did not work. Later, I would sort out the reasons why they were not working for me, and correct the problem. But the details of that story are far afield of the topic at hand. Some aspects of the issue are discussed in the chapter titled *Mystical Practices*.

My intellectual efforts, though they were fascinating to me, still were not yielding results. I ran into many dead ends. But a picture was gradually taking shape. A turning point came when, for the first time, I clearly saw the problem I was trying to solve. I saw the one question which lay behind all of my other questions. Once I knew what I wanted to know, my work sped up significantly.

The problem that I saw was the problem of reconciling mysticism with rationality. Let us now digress from our narrative again, and learn what this problem is.

Rationality is the method of seeking the truth which is exemplified by mathematics and science. It determines truth through evidence and formal reasoning. Mysticism is another method of seeking the truth, which determines truth through direct experience and intuition.

These two had been at war in my head ever since I began practicing mysticism. My rational side was very skeptical of my mystical thoughts, because they could not meet the standards of precise formulation and rigorous justification which rationality demands.

I had seen the power of math and science. I knew that through the methods of rationality, one could arrive at truths so solid that they were practically impossible to doubt. I was also inspired by the fact that rational truths are shareable; when one arrives at a correct proof, everybody can see that it is correct, and there is no controversy about the matter.

The truths of mysticism seemed to me just as solid and impossible to doubt as the truths of rationality. Actually, they seemed vastly more so. So it seemed right to me that they ought to be formulated precisely and rigorously justified, like the truths of rationality. My guiding motivation was my desire to share these truths with others. But mystical truth, as I was discovering, was very hard to formulate in the usual rational fashion. This was just one of my problems.

Another problem was as follows. I had acquired a large and growing collection of mystical beliefs; but, I did not know why I held these beliefs. I could not explain, even to myself, the reasons as to why they were true. This made me wonder whether or not they were true at all. I faced a serious problem of verification.

In short, I found myself unable to state what I believed, and why I believed it. The methods of rationality were the only methods I knew of for articulating and verifying beliefs. So I wished to capture my mystical thinking within a rational framework. This required that I resolve the conflicts which exist between rationality and mysticism. Thus many different problems eventually coalesced in my understanding into the general problem of synthesizing rationality and mysticism.

Around the same time, I was becoming more and more absorbed in the philosophy articulated in the *Law of One* documents, channelled by Carla Ruckert, Don Elkins and Jim McCarty in the 1980s.[1]

To me these documents absolutely moaned with beauty and meaning. They combined the rationality of a math proof with the emotional power of a Beethoven symphony. For months I was lost in the aesthetic rapture of contemplating the *Law of One*.

At some point I gave up on reconciling rationality and mysticism. I decided to damn the torpedoes and conclude that the *Law of One* documents were the literal and absolute truth. I believed in them with a wholeheartedness which I had never before given to any philosophy. This was the status quo for a few months, and my intellectual efforts turned towards working out the details of that system of thought.

In the summer I was revisited by my old friend, doubt. I began to see cracks in the wall. I began to wonder, somewhere in the back of my mind, if perhaps I had fallen into the same trap that so many religious zealots had fallen into before me. It was very quiet at first.

The dam broke when I read the *Less Wrong* sequences, by Eliezer Yudkowsky. These sequences are a presentation of the principles of rationality. Yudkowsky said what I already knew, with such force and clarity that I had to hear it. I could no longer hide myself from the problem. I saw that I had been irrational in accepting the *Law of One* as truth.

---

[1] http://lawofone.info/

INTRODUCTION

I found myself in the most genuine confusion I had ever felt. The rationality/mysticism problem revisited me with painful intensity. My understanding of rationality, and my understanding of mysticism, had both deepened immensely since my last battle with the problem; so the incompatibilities were thrown into violent contrast. For days I experienced nonstop cognitive dissonance, which was sometimes so intense that it became physical pain. But I was rejoicing through the whole process, because I knew that I was coming closer to the truth, and making progress on a problem that few souls had ever penetrated.

Eventually the fireworks died down, and clarity slowly began to emerge. Every so often, another one of the puzzle pieces would coalesce in my thinking. Then one night, the last of the pieces came together, and I saw the solution standing before me, like an angel from heaven. Rejoicing, I excitedly began to write. Within about two weeks, I wrote most of the first seven chapters of this book.

Part One of this book, then, is devoted to solving the conflict between rationality and mysticism. Part Two contains a number of chapters which I wrote earlier in my studies. Chapters Eight and Nine are devoted to explaining certain mystical intuitions. They are followed by a three-chapter sequence titled *Soliloquy on Free Will and the World*, which was an early attempt at combining rationality and mysticism.

The chapters of Part Two lack the rigor of Part One; when I wrote them I had not yet developed my sharp eye for logical consistency. I find their merit to lie mainly in their aesthetic beauty, and in the fact that they explain certain important mystical intuitions.

I wish now to provide you with an explanation for the title of this work. This will require an abrupt shift into the language of mysticism; I apologize if the reader feels any whiplash.

The esoteric meaning of the phrase "eh na?" was explained by William Gray in *Qabalistic Concepts*.[2] "Eh na?" is a Hebrew phrase which, according to Gray, is the root of the Hebrew word "ain" (אין). "Ain" means "nothing." The root phrase "eh na?" is a question, meaning roughly "what now?" It is a request for further understanding.

---

[2] Gray, William. *Qabalistic Concepts*. Chapter 8. pages 102-103

The connection between these two phrases leads to the understanding of nothing as a question. Later we will explore the conception of nothingness as the secret ground of being or heart of reality. Here we consider nothingness as an eternal, unanswerable question, a seeking which can never be completed. The insight that I wish to convey can be seen by regarding these two conceptions of nothing as one, as expressed in the connection of the Hebrew phrases "ain" and "eh na?"

There is only one question, and it has no answer. The one question could be formulated like so: "what is existence?" or "what is this?" or "eh na?" or even just "?" — all different ways of phrasing the one question. All other questions are actually this question, in what we imagine to be different forms: "Who am I?", "What time is it?", "Where am I going to get my next meal?"

All questions, when properly considered, boil down to the one question, or else they are not questions at all. Furthermore, these questions have no answer; the idea that they are ever answered, or that they ever need an answer, is just this illusion that we have.

The question "what now?" — or, "what do I do right now?" or, "how do I live my life?" — is a philosophical question which never ceases to yield fruitful results. It is an infinitely practical question, for the reason that its answer will be relevant at every moment, and we are in fact *required* to answer it at every moment, in that we do in fact implicitly answer it with our every action. In addition to being continually relevant, the question is so expansive that it utterly defies being answered in any definite way; one can make an arbitrary amount of progress on it without ever coming to the end of it.

The world is full of answers to the question posed here. The religions, psychologies, self-help philosophies, etc., all provide their own answers. By the virtue of this very fact we are led to be skeptical of all of these answers; for all of the answers contradict each other, and therefore cancel each other out unless we can find some means of establishing positively that one of them wins out over the others. Either we do this, or we posit that in fact none of them are the answer. Since the necessity of answering the question remains, we are left then to strike out on our own and determine the answer for ourselves.

With this question we feel the contradiction that arises with philosophical questions in general: on the one hand the undeniable centrality of its importance, and on the other hand the utter lack of any clear answer and the immense perplexity that inevitably arises in any attempt to think about it. In such questioning one does not find the answer; rather one progressively increases the depth of one's unknowing. One knows more and more without ever finding the answer.

The meaning of equating nothingness with the question "what now?" is that though we may make progress on the question, we may never finish with the question. If one gives up on the question, it immediately re-poses itself by virtue of the fact that one then has to find something to do other than ask the question. If one supplies an answer to the question, one will find that one's answer leads to new questions. The person who answers the question of life by accepting religion, for instance, does not reduce their questions but only multiplies them, for their religion and their acceptance of it will pose its own plethora of problems.

To solve the question of life is to finish with life; for if one has solved the question of life, one goes no further, but rather fades away into nothingness. Yet this never occurs; we are never finished. Thus we see that nothingness is not a thing, place, or state, as many have supposed — "heaven," "moksha," "nirvana," etc., all being different words for nothingness. These nothingness do not exist; nothingness is simply nonexistence, and it is obvious that nonexistence does not exist. Nothingness, then, is not a thing, place, or state, but the unattainable limit of a process of revelation; in this process, nothingness is precisely the receding horizon of the unrevealed.

Philosophy, being the discipline concerned with exploring the paradoxical and the hazy boundaries of our knowledge, reaches towards nothingness in all of its inquiries. Similarly for mysticism, which is concerned with reaching towards the boundaries of perception, and moving from the familiar ordinary into the unfamiliar extraordinary of life. All human activities which reach towards nothingness acquire by virtue of this a certain commonality, and we may call them "religious" activities in the truest sense. Religious activity, in the truest sense, is the reaching towards nothingness, or put differently, the *inquiring* towards nothingness, the asking of the question of nothingness. It will therefore be appropriate for us to take nothingness as our point of departure into our investigation of mysticism when we look at it in Part Two. Until then, let us delve into the relationship between rationality and mysticism.

PART ONE

A RATIONAL ANALYSIS OF MYSTICISM

EXPLAINING what mysticism is has been an ongoing problem for me. It eludes definition in a most infuriating way. My attempts to explain it have led me to split it into three parts: Mystical Experiences, Mystical Practices, and Mystical Thinking.

All three of these will be discussed in detail in the forthcoming chapters. The majority of the book is devoted to mystical thinking. Mystical thinking is no more important than the other two, but it generates many more words.

Before entering into mystical thinking, we will discuss another, quite different type of thinking: namely, rational thinking, or simply "rationality". What is rationality? For our purposes, it is a method of arriving at true beliefs through systematic reasoning, as exemplified in math and science, and sometimes in philosophy. What does rationality have to do with mysticism? Precisely this: rationality and mysticism are both methods of discovering the truth.

It is my basic assumption that rationality and mysticism are both useful tools for discovering the truth, and that an ideal approach to truth-seeking combines them. I feel that rationality and mysticism correct for each other's weaknesses and are each capable of things that the other is not.

Suppose that a mystic walks up to me and asks, "why should I care about rational thinking?" I can answer them:

- *"With rationality, you can know that your beliefs are true, rather than merely having faith that they are true."*

- *"With rationality, you can notice when you hold a false belief, and stop believing it."*

- *"With rationality, you can gain clear and systematic mental processes which make it easier to think and easier to communicate".*

Now suppose that a rationalist walks up to me and asks, "why should I care about mysticism?" I can answer them:

- *"With mysticism, you can discover truths that rationality cannot discover by itself. These truths primarily have to do with the human mind and the inner life, as opposed to the physical world and the outer life which rationality is best at understanding."*

- *"With these truths, you can improve yourself, improve your life, and become a happier, wiser, and more morally positive person."*

Rationality and mysticism both offer us many benefits. The problem is that there are deep incompatibilities between rationality and mysticism, which result in the two disciplines being quite difficult to reconcile.

The incompatibilities have to do with mystical thinking. The majority of commonly espoused mystical beliefs cannot be justified rationally. Rationality tells us that we should always follow the methods of rationality, such as gathering evidence and forming logical arguments, in deciding our beliefs. It tells us that this is the only way we can be confident that our beliefs are true.

The problem is that there is almost no commonly held mystical belief which can be arrived at through the methods of rationality. On the face of it, therefore, it appears that if we are to adhere strictly to the rules of rationality, we must reject all mystical beliefs.

Being dissatisfied with this situation, I attempted to find a way to reconcile these two conflicting disciplines. I here present my own method of discovering truth, which is an attempt to synthesize rationality and mysticism. It addresses the relationship of rationality to all three aspects of mysticism that we have noted. The thoughts that I present here are the outcome of many experiments in combining these two disciplines.

I would not present my thoughts here as the final and perfect synthesis of the two disciplines; but I believe that I have made significant inroads on the problem. It is my hope that you can use these tools as an aid in discovering truth for yourselves.

"This phenomenon usually comes as a tremendous shock. It is indescribable even by the masters of language; and it is therefore not surprising that semi-educated stutterers wallow in oceans of gush.

All the poetic faculties and all the emotional faculties are thrown into a sort of ecstasy by an occurrence which overthrows the mind, and makes the rest of life seem utterly worthless in comparison."

- Aleister Crowley, Liber ABA

1

MYSTICAL EXPERIENCE

LYING at the heart of mysticism is the mystical experience. Mysticism's basic purpose is to bring about this experience, and so without it, the whole structure collapses. It is important, then, that we ask what a mystical experience is.

From a religious point of view, mystical experiences are commonly interpreted as encounters with the divine, a union with God, or a transcendence to a higher reality. In contrast, the field of psychology studies mystical experiences without superimposing any assumed religious interpretation thereupon. Let us assume the latter interpretive stance for the moment.

Mystical experiences, as a psychological phenomenon, are not universal; it seems that only some people ever have them. That said, they are not extraordinarily uncommon, and probably more common than average among people reading this book.

A mystical experience is a state of consciousness whose common features include altered perceptions; intense, usually positive, emotions; a sense of insight or revelation; and a sense of existential significance to the "experiencer".

Most religious traditions contain their own synonyms for "mystical experience," which include "theosis" in Christian mysticism, "dhyana" or "samadhi" in Hinduism, and "jhana" in Buddhism.[1]

Experiencers generally agree that no adequate linguistic description of mystical experience is possible. This fact has significance for us firstly because it is an important diagnostic criterion of mystical experience,

---

[1] "Dhyana" (Sanskrit) and "jhana" (Pali) are the same term to describe "the union between the meditator and the object of meditation."

and secondly because it means that the list of symptoms which I am about to present will necessarily fail to adequately characterize the nature of mystical experience.

The following description of the components of mystical experience is drawn from an analysis of written reports of mystical experiences by numerous individuals, from *The Mystical Experience Registry*.[2]

The most easily characterized aspects of mystical experience are the emotional aspects. There are usually powerful feelings of ecstasy, bliss, joy, peace, beauty, or love. Sometimes there are negative feelings, such as fear or anguish.

There is usually a sense of increased consciousness, awakeness, or aliveness. The experience often feels subjectively more real than anything in ordinary life.

There may be sensory phenomena, such as bright lights, tingling or other tactile sensations, a feeling of the boundaries dissolving between the body and the environment, or a feeling of having left the body entirely.

There may be auditory hallucinations: usually voices, often interpreted as emanating from a divine entity. There may be visual hallucinations or imagery of various kinds. There may be a sense of a foreign presence, usually interpreted as a divine entity.

There may be an obliteration of the sense of time, space, or self. There may also be time dilation.

There is often a sense of some kind of insight, like a profound truth has been revealed. Experiencers commonly garner ideas of various kinds from their mystical experiences. Most often these ideas are of a philosophical, religious, or moral nature.

Sometimes ideas are dramatically "revealed" in the midst of the experience, appearing as if out of nowhere in the experiencer's mind and being powerfully impressed thereupon. Other times they emerge out of reflection subsequent to the experience.

Ideas drawn from mystical experience will tend to exert a strange sway of authority over the experiencer. The experiencer will often be quite convinced of such an idea's truth, even if the only support for the idea comes from the experience itself.

Those who have mystical experiences generally find them to be of such subjective significance that all other experiences appear pale and meaningless in comparison.

---

[2] http://www.bodysoulandspirit.net/mystical_experiences/index.shtml

Examples of Mystical Experiences

The remainder of this chapter will give descriptions of a number of mystical experiences had by various people. It is my feeling that enumerating these examples will yield a clearer idea of the general character, as well as the diversity, of mystical experiences.

The examples chosen are, by design, more on the dramatic side of things. This is because the dramatic experiences are more illustrative, and also easier to describe, than the subtler experiences. But it is worth noting that not every mystical experience is as over the top as many of these; they can be a quiet affair as well.

1. *"I was meditating on a point between my eyebrows. As I deepened my concentration, my whole being began to be sucked into this point. It was a tunnel into which I was going deeper, and at the end of the tunnel there was a soft, vibrating light. There was a break in my memory. The next thing I remember was floating in a void made of light and consciousness, in a state of totally passionless bliss. This place was completely silent, and far more real, concrete, and tangible than anything in normal experience."*

2. *"Suddenly, at church, or in company, or when I was reading, and always, I think, when my muscles were at rest, I felt the approach of the mood. Irresistibly it took possession of my mind and will, lasted what seemed an eternity, and disappeared in a series of rapid sensations which resembled the awakening from anaesthetic influence. One reason why I disliked this kind of trance was that I could not describe it to myself. I cannot even now find words to render it intelligible. It consisted in a gradual but swiftly progressive obliteration of space, time, sensation, and the multitudinous factors of experience which seem to qualify what we are pleased to call our Self. In proportion as these conditions of ordinary consciousness were subtracted, the sense of an underlying or essential consciousness acquired intensity. At last nothing remained but a pure, absolute, abstract Self. The universe became without form and void of content. But Self persisted, formidable in its vivid keenness, feeling the most poignant doubt about reality, ready, as it seemed, to find existence break as breaks a bubble round about it. And what then? The apprehension of a coming dissolution, the grim conviction that this state was the last state of the conscious Self, the sense that I had followed the last thread of being to the verge of the abyss, and had arrived at demonstration of eternal Maya or illusion, stirred or seemed to stir me up again. The return to ordinary conditions of sentient existence*

began by my first recovering the power of touch, and then by the gradual though rapid influx of familiar impressions and diurnal interests. At last I felt myself once more a human being; and though the riddle of what is meant by life remained unsolved I was thankful for this return from the abyss -- this deliverance from so awful an initiation into the mysteries of skepticism.

This trance recurred with diminishing frequency until I reached the age of twenty-eight. It served to impress upon my growing nature the phantasmal unreality of all the circumstances which contribute to a merely phenomenal consciousness. Often have I asked myself with anguish, on waking from that formless state of denuded, keenly sentient being, Which is the unreality -- the trance of fiery, vacant, apprehensive, skeptical Self from which I issue, or these surrounding phenomena and habits which veil that inner Self and build a self of flesh-and-blood conventionality? Again, are men the factors of some dream, the dream-like insubstantiality of which they comprehend at such eventful moments? What would happen if the final stage of the trance were reached?"[3]

3. *"I was reading the Tractatus Logico-Philosophicus by Ludwig Wittgenstein, and he came to section 6.4311. It states, 'Death is not an event of life. Death is not lived through. If by eternity is understood not endless temporal duration but timelessness, then he lives eternally who lives in the present. Our life is endless in the way that our visual field is without limit.'*[4]

Upon reading this, I began to be enveloped in a strange sense of peace. Everything was still; time had ceased to pass. The next hour was in suspended animation. Though I was moving about and performing activities, it was as if nothing was happening; as if I had never stopped reading that one passage. The whole hour was compressed into a single moment; or, a single moment was stretched across the entire hour. The moment was one of quiet perfection with no possibility of disharmony, past, present, or future."

4. *"With me, as with every other person of whom I have heard, the keynote of the experience is the tremendously exciting sense of an intense metaphysical illumination. Truth lies open to the view in depth beneath depth of almost blinding evidence. The mind sees all logical relations of being with*

---

[3] Brown, H.F. *J.A. Symonds: A Biography*. London, 1895, pp. 29-31, abridged. Quoted in James, William. *Varieties of Religious Experience*. Longmans, Green & Co., London, 1902.

[4] Wittgenstein, Ludwig. *Tractatus Logico-Philosophicus*. German text with an English translation by C.K. Ogden. Routledge and Kegan Paul, London 1922.

an apparent subtlety and instantaneity to which its normal consciousness offers no parallel; only as sobriety returns, the feeling of insight fades, and one is left staring vacantly at a few disjointed words and phrases, as one stares at a cadaverous-looking snow-peak from which sunset glow has just fled, or at a black cinder left by an extinguished brand.

[...]

Whatever the idea of representation occurred to the mind was seized by the same logical forceps, and served to illustrate the same truth; and that truth was that every opposition, among whatsoever things, vanishes in a higher unity in which it is based; that all contradictions, so-called, are of a common kind; that unbroken continuity is of the essence of being; and that we are literally in the midst of an infinite, to perceive the existence of which is the utmost we can attain. Without the same as a basis, how could strife occur? Strife presupposes something to be striven about; and in this common topic, the same for both parties, the differences merge. From the hardest contradiction to the tenderest diversity of verbiage differences evaporate; yes and no agree at least in being assertions; a denial of a statement is but another mode of stating the same, contradictions can only occur of the same thing -- all opinions are thus synonyms, are synonymous, are the same. But the same phrase by different emphasis is two; and here again difference and no-difference merge in one.

It is impossible to convey an idea of the torrential character of the identification of opposites as it streams through the mind in this experience. I have sheet after sheet of phrases dictated or written during the intoxication, which to the sober reader seem meaningless drivel, but which at the moment of transcribing were fused in the fire of infinite rationality. God and devil, good and evil, life and death, I and thou, sober and drunk, matter and form, black and white, quality and quantity, shiver of ecstasy and shudder of horror, vomiting and swallowing, inspiration and expiration, fate and reason, great and small, extent and intent, joke and earnest, tragic and comic, and fifty other contrasts figure in these pages in the same monotonous way. The mind saw how each term belonged to its contrast through a knife-edge moment of transition which it effected, and which, perennial and eternal, was the nunc stans[5] *of life. The thought of mutual implication of the parts in the bare form of a judgement of opposition as 'nothing -- but,' 'no more -- than,' 'Only -- if,' etc., produced a perfect delirium of theoretic rapture."*[6]

---

[5] This Latin phrase, used by James in describing his experience, means "the everlasting Now."

[6] James, William. "Subjective Effects of Nitrous Oxide." *Mind*, Vol.7, 1882

5. *"It was as if I had never realized before how lovely the world was. I lay down on my back in the warm, dry moss and listened to the skylark singing as it mounted up from the fields near the sea into the dark clear sky. No other music ever gave me the same pleasure as that passionately joyous singing. It was a kind of leaping, exultant ecstasy, a bright, flame-like sound, rejoicing in itself. And then a curious experience befell me. It was as if everything that had seemed to be external and around me were suddenly within me. The whole world seemed to be within me. It was within me that the trees waved their green branches, it was within me that the skylark was singing, it was within me that the hot sun shone, and that the shade was cool. A cloud rose in the sky, and passed in a light shower that pattered on the leaves, and I felt its freshness dropping into my soul, and I felt in all my being the delicious fragrance of the earth and the grass and the plants and the rich brown soil. I could have sobbed with joy."*[7]

6. *"I was lying on the bed, listening to music that 'A'*[8] *had written. Colors and shapes began to emanate from 'A', and I had the thought that 'A' was God. A turned into a vast black hole, and I was sucked into the black hole. 'A' was emitting some sort of force, which pressed tangibly on every part of my body, while paradoxically simultaneously pulling. I stayed in the center of the black hole for about an hour, prostrating myself before 'A's' glory."*

7. *"I was walking in nature. I felt myself to be charged with a tremendous power, best described as electrical in nature. The power was radiating out of me and suffusing the whole landscape, which rippled and shimmered in an animated fashion. I felt as if I could have chosen to blow up a car with my mind, if the inclination struck me."*

The foregoing examples illustrate the diverse nature of mystical experiences. Yet it may also be possible to see, even with these few examples, the thematic unity which ties mystical experiences together. This commonality is more difficult to articulate than the distinctions; but every mystic will agree that there is a common content and subject matter to every mystical experience.

It has unfortunately been my experience that those who have not actually had mystical experiences consistently fail to understand what a mystical experience is. Nor should we find this to be particularly

---

[7] Reid, Forrest. *Following Darkness*. London: Arnold, 1902.

[8] "A" is an individual who was present at the time of the experience.

remarkable; it is true of experiences in general that their qualities cannot be conveyed in words to one without an appropriate point of reference. One cannot explain the taste of a mango to somebody who has not tasted a mango. One who has never been drunk cannot successfully imagine the feeling of drunkenness. An explanation such as this chapter, therefore, can only go so far. Unfortunately, it seems to be impossible to give a genuine explanation of this phenomenon, which would cause one who did not already understand it to begin to understand it.

"Without sensibility no object would be given to us, and without understanding none would be thought.

Thoughts without content are empty, intuitions without concepts are blind."

- Kant, Critique of Pure Reason

2

LOGIC AND EXPERIENCE

WESTERN philosophy, since its beginning, has been concerned with the distinction between two sources of knowledge: logic[1], and experience. Ancient Greek philosophers, beginning with the Presocratics, discussed the distinction between logos (λόγος) and empeiria (ἐμπειρία), generally translated as "reason" and "experience." Logos seems to have meant to them, what is directly knowable through the mind and the intellect; whereas empeiria meant things such as sensory experience, emotions, and cultural conditioning. The Ancient Greek philosophers believed that reason was the true source of knowledge, and that experience was a misleading source of error.

This seed idea from the Greeks led to a long-standing debate in Western philosophy between the rationalists, who favored reason as a superior source of knowledge, and the empiricists, who favored experience as a superior source of knowledge. These two beliefs were associated with significantly divergent styles of philosophy. Modern philosophy has moved beyond this debate, having gained a clearer understanding of how reason and experience work together to give rise to our knowledge.

The distinction between reason and experience has meant many different things to different people at different times. That said, a certain core of meaning remains constant. This core of meaning could be described as follows. Reason encompasses what we can know

---

[1] A more common term for this concept is "reason," but I prefer "logic" due to the confusion that would otherwise arise between the word "reason" and the word "rationality."

with our intellect. Experience encompasses what we know through our non-intellectual faculties, such as our senses.

The distinction between reason and experience is of central importance for our project, in that it is the cornerstone of my strategy for reconciling rationality and mysticism. Therefore, before proceeding, I wish to make as clear and vivid as possible the distinction between reason and experience as I mean it. However, I will use the word "logic" instead of "reason," because I wish to avoid confusion with the concept of rationality.

By "logic" and "experience," I mean two facets of the human mind. They are psychological terms. Logic is the faculty of manipulating symbols, positing logical relations, computing, and calculating. Experience is most neatly defined as every conscious aspect of the human mind that is not logic. Thus it includes our five senses, our emotions, and our intuitions. Since experience is defined as that which is not logic, together the two terms encompass every conscious aspect of the human mind.

Every logical idea can be articulated as a mathematical expression. Thus logic takes in mathematics itself, science, and most technical disciplines, such as engineering or computer science.

In addition, much of the content of everyday thought is logical. As Bertrand Russell observed, ordinary sentences can generally be rephrased as mathematical expressions, in the mathematical language called formal logic.

For instance, suppose I say: *"The bus runs every hour, on the hour, and the last bus runs at midnight."* This could be written in formal logic as follows:

$$(T - \text{floor}(T) = 0 \land T \leq 12) \to R(B)$$

"T" is the current time, in hours, as a real number. "T - floor(T) = 0" is a translation of, "the current time is on the hour." "R(B)" is a translation of, "the bus runs." The whole statement can thus be read, "if the current time is on the hour, and ($\land$) the current time is less than or equal to twelve, then the bus runs."

It is rather easy to take any statement and re-write it in formal logic. Thus we are led to the potentially surprising conclusion that everything we say has a logical structure and a logical meaning, which can be expressed in a simple mathematical language.

Bertrand Russell attempted to create systematic methods by which any English sentence could be rephrased in formal logic.

Seemingly, he came very close to doing this. However, Russell's project ultimately failed, due to the fact that English grammar and semantics do not follow consistent rules.

A deeper problem with his project is the fact that what people mean by sentences is not always logical. For instance, it is difficult to state the logical meaning of utterance, "oh my God!" There is no doubt that we can come up with some scheme by which this and similar utterances can be translated into formal logic; but intuitively, we feel that we have lost something by doing so. There is something in the meaning of that utterance which is not a logical proposition. It expresses an emotional state. Its meaning is experiential, not logical.

That part of a sentence's meaning which is preserved when we re-write it in formal logic, is the logical meaning of the sentence. The experiential meaning is that which is lost when we re-write the sentence in formal logic. It is that to which there is no corresponding mathematical expression.

Emotional states are an example of something genuinely experiential: that is, lying outside the boundaries of logic. Sensations are another example. The idea that sensations are experiential is commonly illustrated in philosophy through the following allegory, first told by Frank Jackson in 1982.[2, 3]

Consider a person, Mary, who has lived her entire life in a completely colorless room, containing only colorless things. She has working color vision, but she never sees color. She has a computer with a black and white monitor, and on this computer she studies color. She is versed in the science of optics, the workings of the human eye, and color theory. But, she has never seen color.

We would tend to say that Mary's knowledge of color is incomplete. There is something that there is to know about color which Mary does not know, and which she can only come to know by seeing colored things. Through her learning she has acquired extensive logical knowledge of color. But, there is an additional experiential knowledge of color which she lacks, and which is not reducible to any possible logical knowledge of color. This, the colorfulness of color, is an example of something lying outside the boundaries of logic.

---

[2] Jackson, Frank. "Epiphenomenal Qualia." The Philosophical Quarterly 32.127 (1982): 127.

[3] Jackson's line of thought, however, differed from the one I present here. He took his allegory as demonstrating that materialism is false; but I do not draw this conclusion from the allegory.

Now consider somebody looking at a grass lawn. Logically, they can know the species and genus of the grass; they can know that the grass is made of cells, and that it synthesizes food from the sun using chlorophyll; they can know the history of grass lawns as a common feature of middle-class homes; they can know the geometric shapes of the blades of grass. Experientially, they can see the grass; they can feel it between their toes; they can feel a sense of peace and relaxation; they can be bothered by the fact that it is not cut. Together, logic and experience encapsulate all of the ways in which the person can come into relation with the grass lawn.[4]

Reductionism

Some readers will object to the distinction I have made between logic and experience, due to their impression that I am implying that reductionism is false. In order to defuse this objection, I must state what reductionism is, state the apparent conflict, and state why there is in fact no conflict.

Reductionists believe that everything that is true about the universe can be stated logically, in terms of math and science. For example, consider a salt shaker. It is made of glass; it has an aluminium top; and it is filled with salt. We can state the chemical composition of each of these parts, and the spatial/geometric relations which they bear to each other. The salt, for example, is a number of crystals of sodium chloride molecules. A sodium chloride molecule can be described quite precisely as a certain arrangement of subatomic particles, and the relations between the different molecules, in the crystal structure which they form, can be described similarly precisely.

Ultimately, we can reduce everything that is true about the salt shaker to these mathematical relations between its various parts. In fact, everything that is true about the salt shaker can be reduced to what is true about the subatomic particles that make it up. This is the principle of reductionism.

According to reductionism, there is a mathematical formula which completely describes the salt shaker. Furthermore, there is

---

[4] This should not be surprising; it is a tautology. Experience is defined as that which is not logic. Together, therefore, they encapsulate both logic and non-logic — in other words, the entire possibility space.

such a mathematical formula for everything in the universe — up to and including the universe itself. Thus, under reductionism, the universe is reducible to a mathematical formula.

Reductionism is supported by the entire thrust of science. Working under this guiding principle, science has been able to shed light on every aspect of the physical world, and this understanding has enabled the massive technological progress which has occurred in the past few centuries. It is impossible to make sense of science's discoveries without the concept of reductionism, and every practical success of science therefore validates reductionism.

That said, reductionism remains controversial. Some people believe that the validity of reductionism ends at some point. For instance, a person who believes in God is also likely to believe that God is not reducible to a mathematical formula.

The greatest controversy has to do with whether or not reductionism applies to living things, to mental states, and to consciousness. Some people find it hard to believe that people and their experiences are reducible to any kind of mathematical formula.

According to the reductionists, every mental state corresponds to some neurological event in a brain. Thus, an experience of the color red, or an experience of pain, corresponds to some collection of neurons firing. The relationship is one of equality; the experience is the neurons firing. They are one and the same.

This idea is, for many people, about as confusing as the idea that God is three things which are *one* thing. Many people find this idea completely plausible whilst others find it completely implausible.

It requires a serious stretch of the imagination to really wrap one's head around the idea that a subjective experience *is* a set of neurons firing. Probably many of the people who believe in reductionism have never genuinely tried to imagine what this might mean. Of course, the intuitive difficulties which exist with the idea do not mean that it is false.

I do not intend to stake a position either for or against reductionism. I have stated the arguments for it, and the arguments against it. It is not necessary to our purpose to resolve the debate; nor do I think that I can.

The reason I bring up reductionism is that it will seem to some people that my comments on the logic/experience distinction are in conflict with reductionism. In fact, however, they are not.

The apparent conflict is as follows: According to reductionism, the universe is reducible to a mathematical formula. Thus, everything that is true about the universe can be stated logically and there is nothing that falls outside the domain of logic. Even those things which we have called "experiential" — emotions, sensations, etc., — are ultimately logical things which only subjectively feel otherwise.

Consider again the utterance "oh my God!" I said before that this utterance has no logical meaning. Under reductionism, however, we could say what this sentence means by writing out the mathematical formula corresponding to the neurological state of the person uttering the sentence, which caused them to utter the sentence.

Reductionists believe that there is nothing outside of logic. On these grounds, they might reject the logic/experience distinction. This, however, would be based on a misunderstanding of what I am saying by making the distinction. My point is not about the objective nature of things, but about the *subjective way* that humans understand things.

When I refer to the domain of experience, I am not insisting (though it may be so) that the world contains things which are objectively irreducible to logical terms. Minimally, I am pointing out a feature of human psychology: that there are things which we apprehend in a non-logical manner, which we feel rather than calculate. I do not insist on the objectivity of the logic/experience distinction; it may be a distinction that exists only in human subjectivity.

When I say that the meaning of "oh my God!" is experiential and not logical, I am not asserting anything about the reducibility of the mental state which it expresses. I do not mean that it belongs to some objectively non-logical realm of pure experience outside all possible quantification and scientific study. This may be true; but I do not insist that it is so. Rather, I insist that humans understand the utterance through feeling, rather than through reasoning. Thus the logic/experience distinction is psychological, and may or may not be metaphysical.

Reconciling Rationality and Mysticism

It is now possible to state my strategy for reconciling rationality and mysticism. I will present the broad outline here and the subsequent chapters will supply the various details and refinements.

There exists a conflict between rationality and mysticism because both disciplines give us advice about what to believe, and about how to determine our beliefs. Rationality tells us to believe only what we can determine through logical reasoning and the evidence of our senses. Mysticism tells us that there are additional truths which we can arrive at through intuition and mystical experience, which go beyond what reasoning and sense experience can tell us. Thus the incompatibility arises.

Rationality is a corpus of accumulated wisdom for dealing with the domain of logic. It tells us everything about how to think within the domain of logic, and nothing about how to think outside the domain of logic. Rationality is entirely logical.

Mysticism, in contrast, is mostly experiential. Most of mysticism lies in the domain of experience. These parts of mysticism do not conflict with rationality. There is no conflict, for instance, between rationality and a mystical experience consisting of overwhelming joy. Joy does not imply any logical proposition; nor does any logical proposition tell us anything about joy. There is no conflict between rationality and joy because the two do not come into relation with each other.

As previously stated, rationality and mysticism only come into conflict in the context of mystical thinking. We can sharpen this claim by noting that they only come into conflict when mystical thinking is logical.

For instance, suppose that I believe that the Egyptian pyramids were thought into existence by extraterrestrials from Venus.[5] This belief is in the domain of logic; therefore, I must hold it to the standards of rationality. I must be able to justify the belief in the ordinary way. If I cannot do this, then I must abandon the belief.

Mysticism could greatly increase its credibility by adhering to this simple standard: claims in the domain of logic must meet the criteria of rationality. This standard forces us to throw a great proportion of mystical ideas out the window.

Later we shall find reason to adjust this standard somewhat; that is, we will find reason to deviate from the established criteria of rationality. But the criteria of rationality will be our starting point for deciding our logical beliefs.

---

5 This claim can be found in the Law of One documents, published by L/L Research.

As the reader may have guessed, many mystical ideas are not in the domain of logic, but in the domain of experience. Consider, for instance, the concept of universal love. Logically speaking, we are at a loss for what the phrase "universal love" even means. The concept is an experiential one, for which we cannot give a logical explanation. "Universal love" can be understood by one who has felt, or can imagine feeling, universal love.

Other mystical ideas seem to tread delicately the line between logic and experience. If we try to interpret them logically, we can produce a logical interpretation. If we try to interpret them experientially, we can produce an experiential interpretation.

Consider, for instance, the phrase "in God, all things are possible." Let us attempt to produce a logical interpretation. "All things" can clearly be interpreted logically, as can "possible." The main sticking point is "in God." What is "God," and what does it mean to be "in" it?

Perhaps we take the sentence as meaning that one who is sufficiently in harmony with God can literally do anything. Naturally, we would have to hold such a belief to the standards of rationality — and we still have yet to specify what we mean by "God."

So what do we mean by God? Is God a force? A person? An intelligence? Where is it located? What is it shaped like? How much does it weigh? My questions are deliberately chosen to seem ridiculous. If we wish to ascribe a logical meaning to the word "God," we must confront such questions; and this in itself suggests that we are on the wrong path.

We can, alternatively, interpret the word "God" as having no logical meaning whatsoever. We can interpret it as having only experiential meaning. We can then postulate that this experiential meaning is to be apprehended through mystical experience.

We can apply the same strategy in order to achieve a more satisfactory interpretation of the phrase "in God, all things are possible." We may take this phrase as implying no logical proposition. God does not give us infinite possibilities in any material, worldly sense. We have the same material possibilities with God as we would have without God. But, in a purely experiential sense, with God we have infinite possibility.

Mystical statements, interpreted logically, almost always fail to meet the standards of rationality. If we wish to adhere to these standards, therefore, we must discard almost all logical interpretations of mystical ideas. When mystical statements are interpreted experientially, however, they are removed from any possibility of rational criticism.

I am of the opinion that most of what is of value in mysticism is in the domain of experience, rather than in the domain of logic. So, by discarding logical interpretations of mystical ideas, we lose very little of value. Interpreted logically, mystical ideas are usually false or nonsensical. Interpreted experientially, they are often very profound.

Thus, my strategy for reconciling rationality and mysticism consists mostly of discarding logical interpretations of mystical ideas. In the following chapters, I will offer further refinements to this basic concept.

"A burning itch to know is higher than a solemn vow to pursue truth. To feel the burning itch of curiosity requires both that you be ignorant, and that you desire to relinquish your ignorance."

- Eliezer Yudkowsky, "The Twelve Virtues of Rationality"

3

RATIONALITY

WHAT is rationality, and how do we think rationally? As with many complex concepts, there is no quote, no sound bite or no bumper-sticker slogan which can accurately summarize rationality. For our purposes, it is a way of seeking the truth. In particular, it is the way of the seeking the truth that is practiced in science, mathematics, and some types of philosophy.[1]

Rationality bears an essential relationship to logic. Logic is a mental faculty and rationality is the correct way to use that faculty. Unfortunately, since rationality is a complex set of mental habits and skills, it really is impossible to boil down rationality to anything that can be contained in a series of pages.

In fact, you probably already know most of the components of rationality. For example, you might already know how to form a logical argument, a scientific or mathematical method, be able to notice a contradiction or identify some faulty reasoning. So this chapter will only, shall we say, put the icing on the cake.

Truth

Rationality is about seeking the truth. It tells us how to distinguish true beliefs from false beliefs, and how to uncover the truth when it is unknown. Thus we believe that rationality leads

---

[1] There are two major divisions in modern philosophy: analytic, and continental. Analytic philosophy almost always adheres to rationality; continental philosophy almost never does so.

us to the truth. But what is truth? There is a great deal of confusion surrounding this word. In recent years, particularly, one can find two fairly odd claims: that "truth is relative," and that "truth does not exist."

If either of these claims is true,[2] then rationality cannot fulfill the hopes which we had for it. If truth does not exist, then rationality cannot lead us to the truth. If the truth is relative, then we face a similar problem. Rationality claims that its truths are independent of humans, and not a matter of opinion. Two people cannot disagree, for instance, on whether or not there is an infinite quantity of prime numbers; and if nobody had ever discovered that there is an infinite quantity of prime numbers, it would still be the case that there is.

If "truth does not exist" or if "truth is relative," then rationality loses its status as a source of truth. This would mean that our project to reconcile rationality and mysticism was misguided and useless. The conflict between these two arises from the fact that both claim to reveal the truth to us, but the beliefs they provide us with, and the means of determining those beliefs, are inconsistent. The conflict arises from the purported objectivity of both disciplines. If rational beliefs and mystical beliefs are both untrue, or both merely relatively true, then there is really nothing to reconcile.

So, let us ask: "does truth exist, and is it relative?" We find ourselves back at our original question: what is truth? This question, however, baffles us with a dazzling sense of mystery. It is so abstract and stupendous that we simply have no idea where to start. Let us first try, then, to answer an easier question. Let us consider how the concept of truth is used in everyday life.

Suppose I say, "it is true that it is raining outside." What does this mean? It means that it is raining outside. To make the point clearer, and dismiss the impression that we are playing word games, let us step away from the language we are using. I could express the same thing by drawing a picture of what is outside, then drawing clouds above it and filling the foreground with blue droplets. Then I could point to this picture and say, "this is what the world is like."

---

[2] No snickering, please, about the logical paradoxes which arise from saying that either of these things are "true!" (If nothing is true, then it cannot be true that nothing is true. And if truth is relative, then it can only be relatively true that truth is relative.)

Suppose that I say that "it is true that two plus two equals four." What do I mean by this? I mean many things. I mean that if I punched the formula "2 + 2" into a calculator, I would expect to get back "4." I mean that if I am with my friend Bob, and we run into our friends Jane and Jill, and then I point at each one of us in turn while counting up from one, the last thing I will say is "four." I mean that if I have two dollars, and then I am given two more dollars, I still cannot buy something that is priced at five dollars.

Suppose I say that "it is true that $F = ma$." What do I mean by this? I mean many things. One of the things I mean is that, if one builds a rocket while making use of this equation, that rocket has a chance of getting to the moon; whereas, if one builds a rocket while making use of the equation "$F = m/a$," that rocket has no chance of getting to the moon.

Now we have some understanding of what we mean by "true." So what does a person mean when they say that "truth is relative," or "truth does not exist?" Surely they do not mean, that if they punch "2 + 2" into their calculator, they will get back anything other than "4." Surely they do not mean, that one cannot use the equation "$F = ma$" to build a rocket, or that one *can* use the equation "$F = m/a$" to build a rocket. Surely they do not mean, that if they have two dollars and I give them two more dollars, they might be able to buy something priced at five dollars.

In the ordinary course of life, they act as if, and even think as if, these things that I call *true* really are true. Probably if I ask them by surprise, when their philosophical views of truth aren't on their mind, "is it true that smoking causes lung cancer?" they will respond, "yes, it is true." So what *do* they mean when they say that "truth is relative," or that "truth does not exist?" Why did people begin uttering these sentences? There are, in fact, legitimate and interesting facts that have led people to begin uttering these sentences. Let us then take a survey of these facts.

We may notice, firstly, the problem of skepticism. The problem of skepticism is that we cannot know anything to be true for certain. Scientific theories are based on empirical data, and may be (often are) refuted when further data is gathered. Mathematical truths follow logically from the axioms in which they are based; but we do not, and cannot, have any proof that the axioms themselves are true. All of science is based on the concept of causality, but after centuries of philosophers working on the problem, we still do not know what a "cause" is or whether there is such a thing. Due to the problem of induction, we cannot know whether or not the sun will rise tomorrow. As Eliezer Yudkowsky pointed out,[3] it may be that there are bugs in the human nervous system which cause all of us to be completely and unshakably oblivious to some basic facts about the world. This is a brief survey of some skeptical problems; but we could spend many pages rattling off the various challenges that exist to our having certainty about anything.

It is my opinion that the problem of skepticism is real, and that we genuinely cannot be certain about anything. (I am not certain of this; I am merely very confident.) Since we cannot be certain of anything, we can only think in terms of degrees of confidence.

The problem of skepticism in no way implies either that truth is relative, or that truth does not exist. The confusion seems to be as follows: One takes the problem of skepticism as meaning that humans do not know the truth. One then proceeds from "humans do not know the truth" to "the truth does not exist" — which does not follow. Even when humans did not know that there is an infinite quantity of prime numbers, it was still the case that there is an infinite quantity of prime numbers.

The problem of skepticism is only a part of why people say that "truth does not exist" and that "truth is relative." The distinction between logic and experience can help us to untangle the rest of the problem.

The types of cases that we have considered so far have all been in the domain of logic. Whether it is raining outside, whether 2+2=4, whether F=ma, and whether smoking causes lung cancer are all matters of logic. Furthermore, they are all things that are very clear-cut, and it seems undeniable that they are true in some sense or another.

I suggest that this type of clear-cut, indisputable distinction between true and false is specifically a feature of the domain of logic, and that we do not find such a distinction in the domain of experience. The type of truth which definitely exists and is not relative is a logical truth, rather than an experiential truth.

The demands of logical consistency are such that all logical truths stand or fall together. One can say that it is not true that there is an infinite quantity of prime numbers; but only by rejecting

---

3 http://lesswrong.com/lw/12s/the_strangest_thing_an_ai_could_tell_you/

the truth of the entirety of mathematics. On the other hand, if one admits the truth of a small portion of mathematics, one then faces the logical necessity of admitting the truth of the entirety of mathematics. It is not possible to reject mathematical truths piecemeal; one can reject any mathematical truth only by rejecting all mathematical truths.

This quality of tightly knit interdependence extends, to a great extent, to all of the logical beliefs that we hold. If one wishes to say, for instance, that phosphorous is not flammable, one must then say that it is impossible to light a cigarette using a match. If one wishes to say that the moon is made of green cheese, one must adjust one's predictions about the volume of the tides, to be consistent with the different mass which the moon would have if it were made of green cheese.

The totality of logical beliefs which we hold, therefore, to a great extent stands or falls as a unit. We cannot change one fact without changing all of the facts. We cannot reject one fact without rejecting all of the facts. For any given meaning of the word "*true*," either all of our logical beliefs are true, or none of them are true. This very fact suggests that there is a sense in which they are true.

There is a certain meaning of the word "true," which leads me to expect to see "4" if I punch "2+2" into a calculator, to be able to build a rocket with the equation "$F=ma$," and so forth. According to this meaning of "*true*," truth exists and is not relative. Perhaps there is some other meaning to the word "true," according to which $F=ma$ is not true; but according to that meaning, no logical belief is true.

So, there is something deserving of the name "truth", which exists and is not relative. Let us call this *truth**. We say that "2+2=4 is *true**," "it is *true** that smoking causes lung cancer," and so forth. Anybody who says that "nothing is true" or "truth is relative" is simply mistaken and confused. If there is anything to these statements, then they cannot be talking about *truth**. They must be talking about something else.

I suggest that there are senses of the word "true," according to which truth may not exist, or may be relative. However, these senses lie in the domain of experience, rather than the domain of logic. There are matters of opinion, of taste, and perhaps of faith, for which these statements may apply. For instance, is there an objective fact of the matter about whether or not corsets are attractive? It seems not.

The ideas that "truth does not exist" and that "truth is relative" are frequently brought up in connection with religion and spirituality. Since these areas are so close to our subject of interest, it is worth our time to ask why.

The most relevant fact that we notice upon turning to religion and spirituality is the fact that countless different doctrines prevail in these fields, all contradicting each other, and all firmly believed by some.

It is impossible that everybody is right in these cases. But it also seems impossible to some that everybody is wrong. To resolve this conflict, the believer that "truth is relative" says that perhaps every person is right for themselves, though they are not right for anybody else. Everybody has their own truth, and there is no fact of the matter.

Why do people say that "truth does not exist?" One sees all of the contradictory answers in this field, and concludes that all of them are wrong. This much is reasonable; the only misstep is in going from "we do not know the truth" to "the truth does not exist." Later it will become clear why this is a misstep.

It seems to me that both of these attitudes often are not so much coherent, rigorously thought out epistemic positions, as ways of escaping the question. One may come to these conclusions to avoid thinking. These beliefs are very handy ways of escaping the work of actually evaluating an issue in detail.

With "truth is relative" there is another possible factor of wishing to be accepting and open-minded. It is not pleasant to disagree with people, and when the truth is unclear, one almost inevitably has to disagree with a lot of people. If one declares that truth is relative, then one can agree with everybody.

So, is there a single truth, in the field of religion and spirituality? Let us examine. First, consider the claim, "Jesus was resurrected three days after dying on the cross." For the purposes of this discussion, let us take this claim completely literally, and not as a metaphor. Is the claim true or false?

Some would say it is definitely true, and some would say that it is definitely false. Perhaps we do not know for sure, because we do not have adequate historical evidence to decide one way or the other. I suggest simply that there *is* a fact of the matter. Either the believers are right, and the skeptics are wrong, or the skeptics are right, and the believers are wrong.

Exactly 500 years ago, to the very minute, at the spot I am sitting while I write this, either a wombat defecated, or a wombat did not defecate. I will never know which of these is true — but one of them is true.

Similarly, either Jesus was resurrected, or Jesus was not resurrected. There is a fact of the matter, even if we do not know what that fact of the matter is.

To see that this must be so, consider the following claim: "Jacques Derrida's great-grandfather came back to life three days after he died." This case is precisely like the case with Jesus, except that religion has nothing to do with it. Now in this case, is there any temptation to say that there is no truth of the matter, or that the truth of the matter is relative? None at all.

There is only one reason that, in the case of Jesus, it is not clear that there is a truth of the matter. This is that our minds are hopelessly muddled on the topic of religion.

Now let us consider the question of the afterlife. Either I will exist after I die, or I will not exist after I die. When I die, I will keep on experiencing something in some non-physical world — or I will not. There is a fact of the matter on this question, and we do not know what that fact of the matter is. When I die, if there is an afterlife, at that time I will know that there is an afterlife. So how can it be that there is not a fact of the matter, if in one possible future I will actually *know* the fact of the matter?

Now consider the question of the soul. Do we, or do we not, have a soul, or some part of our selves which is separate and distinct from our brain and physical body? I suggest that this is another case where there is a fact of the matter. In fact, we may actually know the fact of the matter before we die.

Scientists are currently working towards constructing a computer simulation of a human brain. If we have no souls, and are nothing more than our physical bodies, then such a simulation is possible. One simply has to take the math which the universe performs to actually create our brains, and do that math in a computer. The resulting simulation will behave exactly like a human, and even have conscious, subjective experiences.

If we have souls, or are more than our physical bodies, then such a simulation will not work. The simulation will not behave like a human or have subjective experiences. This is because it will only be simulating the brain without simulating the soul.

There are various qualifiers to this line of thinking, which unfortunately this margin is too small to contain. The bottom line is that, within our lifetimes, we may have experimental evidence which conclusively settles the ancient question of whether or not we have souls.

Now imagine that some time in the future — possibly the very distant future — we do know conclusively whether or not we have souls. Presumably in this future, we will look back on our history, where we said that the answer to the soul question was unknowable, or that the truth about the soul question was relative, and scoff.

To make the point even clearer, imagine a world, otherwise identical to our own, in which our astronomy is much less advanced than it is. We know virtually nothing about the cosmos. In particular, we do not know whether the Sun revolves around the Earth, or the Earth around the Sun.

Furthermore, in this world the Bible says (as it does), that the Sun revolves around the Earth. But, the Qu'ran says that the Earth revolves around the Sun. There is therefore a great religious controversy between the geocentric model and the heliocentric model.

Some individuals throw their hands up in despair, concluding that the nature of the cosmos is an unknowable, unsolvable mystery. Other individuals believe that for Christians, the Sun revolves around the Earth, while for Muslims, the Earth revolves around the Sun. Both the relativists and the unknowable-mystery-ists are wrong. There is a truth of the matter. The truth is that the Earth revolves around the Sun.

Perhaps in the future we will know, with definite certainty, the answer to many of the currently unsolved metaphysical questions. Perhaps the truth will turn out to be quite different from what anybody expected. And even if we never know the answers, it does not follow that there are no answers. There are many questions whose answers we will never know, but which nonetheless definitely have answers.

So for some of the questions of religion and spirituality, there is a fact of the matter, and we do not know what the fact of the matter is. The question is not, "do humans know the truth?", or even "will humans ever know the truth?" The question is really, "would an omniscient being know the truth?" Would an omniscient being know whether or not Jesus was resurrected, whether or not we have souls, and what happens after we die? It's not a trick question.

But we cannot resolve all of the perplexities of religion and spirituality using this technique. Not all claims of religion and spirituality are simply true or false. The claims that are not simply true or false are those claims whose meaning is not logical, but experiential. We will analyze some such classes of claims in the chapter titled *Mystical Thinking*. For now, we will stick to generalities.

Consider the claim, "Jesus Christ is our Lord and Saviour." What does this claim mean? It may mean, "believing in Jesus Christ will send you to heaven." If so, then it is a logical claim, and there is a fact of matter regarding it.

It may mean, "Jesus Christ is the Son of God." If so, then we cannot evaluate the claim until we know exactly what it means to be "the Son of God." Did he have half of God's DNA? Was he perfect like God? (What does it mean to be "perfect?") Was he of two natures, God and human, or of one nature, both human and God? Or, perhaps the statement has no logical meaning?

Alternatively, the claim may mean simply, "Jesus is awesome." If so, then the claim is experiential, and there is no fact of the matter regarding it.

Our two statements, then, have their domain of applicability. However, it is confused and confusing to extend them outside of this domain. Furthermore, this domain is not the domain of rationality. Rationality deals strictly with logical beliefs; it has nothing to say about matters of experience. In the beliefs with which rationality deals, truth and falsehood are clear-cut and not a matter of opinion.

Hopefully the foregoing comments have untangled any confusions the reader may have had surrounding the concept of truth. It was necessary to discuss this issue, because the belief that there is a truth strikes to the core of what rationality is about. Rationality is about seeking the truth. Having established that this goal is not misguided, and having oriented ourselves toward it, let us now consider how to seek the truth.

JUSTIFICATION

We will now consider a principle of rationality so fundamental that a rationalist may not even think of it if asked to define rationality. This principle is that a rational person should be able to justify their beliefs. To justify a belief is to provide an argument which can convince other people that it is true.

Ideally, a belief is justified so well that almost anybody who hears the argument will be convinced of the belief. However, it is not possible to justify a belief so well that *everybody* will agree with it. For every possible claim, there is somebody who will disagree, and one has no guarantee of being able to bring them around.

So, we should not shoot for being absolutely convincing, but only for being so convincing that only people who are pathologically deluded or deeply confused will disagree with us.

The basic measure of how well a belief is justified is the power of one's arguments to convince. If a significant fraction of people disagree with your belief, this is reason to examine the issue more closely. If you cannot convince them, it may be that they see something that you do not.

Science and mathematics have formalized methods of creating convincing arguments. In science, one follows the scientific method. In mathematics, one writes a proof.

When a solid scientific theory is discovered, over time it comes to be the case that almost everybody agrees with it. When a solid mathematical theorem is discovered, everybody who reads the proof immediately agrees with it. So, the scientific and mathematical methods of inquiry are very good at convincing people of newly discovered true beliefs.

But, the methods of math and science are only elaborations of the more basic method of coming up with convincing arguments. In math and science, this is still the objective; the only thing that is different is that in these fields there are systematic ways of coming up with convincing arguments.

Why should we have to justify? This is an interesting question. Obviously, it feels good to be able to convince other people of one's beliefs, but this does not seem like the right motive. Rather we want to be able to justify our beliefs because if we can successfully justify a belief, this means that the belief is probably true.

Ideally, given two intelligent people looking at the same world, those people will be able to agree on how that world is. If they cannot agree on how the world is on a particular issue, then this indicates that at least one of them is wrong or confused. So rational people, like all people, prefer to agree. Having other people agree with me increases my confidence that my beliefs are true.

Ideally, this would not be the case. A perfectly rational person would have their beliefs so well formulated that they would not need others' agreement to validate their beliefs. But, observe that the perfectly rational person would also be able to give a watertight justification for every one of their beliefs. It is only because they already know that they could get others to agree with them if necessary, that they do not need others to in fact agree with them.

If almost everybody agrees with me, this does not indicate for sure that my beliefs are true. But it does indicate either that my beliefs are true, or that they are false in a way that I am unlikely to be able to discover. For practical purposes, if almost everybody agrees with me, then I can almost always be confident in my belief.

If some people disagree with me, however, this casts doubt on my belief. Why is this? If two people disagree, then at least one of them is wrong or confused. All things being equal, I have no reason to believe that it is the other person who is wrong or confused, and not me. It may be that I am missing something that the other person sees; and if this is so, I want to find out what I am missing.

Ideally, when a disagreement exists, one discusses the issue until disagreement no longer exists. One turns the disagreement into agreement. This sometimes happen by one side convincing the other side, but other times it happens by discovering a miscommunication, or coming to agree that neither party's answer is right, or by discovering that the question itself is in some way mistaken. If one cannot eliminate the disagreement, then one is left with the aforementioned problem: at least one person is wrong or confused.

So agreement, or the power to produce agreement, is a basic currency in rationality. We must possess this currency in order to have confidence that our beliefs are true. This currency mostly comes in the form of justification. And that is why we should justify our beliefs whenever possible.

Belief

I once spoke to a Christian who told me that he believed in Christianity, but he did not want to say that it was true, because he knew that he was fallible and his knowledge was limited. I was rather confused about what it might mean to believe something without thinking that it was true.

What does it mean to believe something? Minimally, if I say "I believe X," I should also be willing to say, "X is true, to the best of my knowledge." Belief and truth are not separable concepts; if you are being consistent with yourself, then believing something is necessarily believing that it is true.[4]

There are probably many Christians who say that they believe in Christianity, but who do not actually believe in Christianity. For instance, if a person really believed that non-Christians were to spend infinite time being tortured in hell after death, they would probably put more efforts into proselytizing than the typical Christian does.

We will do well to avoid this sort of believing in things without believing in them. We ought to actually believe what we ostensibly believe; and if there is any discomfort in the thought of actually believing these things, then we ought to ask ourselves whether or not they are true at all.

Skepticism

A basic principle of rationality is that one should be skeptical. To be skeptical is to doubt the things that one hears, and to doubt the things that one thinks.

Why doubt? What advantages does it bring? Let us consider an analogy. Suppose that one is designing a bridge. It is very important that this bridge does not fall. One comes up with a design. At this point, one does not step back and say, "What a lovely design! I am sure that it will not fall down! I have great faith in this design!" An engineer who did this would be a terrible engineer. Instead the engineer asks, "can I find any flaws in this design?" When they find flaws, they fix them. When they can no longer find any flaws, their work is done.

It is the same for constructing a belief system. One does not construct a sound belief system by coming up with some ideas, and then sitting around feeling good about them. Rather, one constructs a sound belief system by coming up with some ideas, looking for any possible flaws in them, fixing the flaws, and continuing until no more flaws are visible. In this manner one maximizes the likelihood that one's beliefs are true and not false.

---

[4] Think of the nonsensical nature of Moore's paradox. Moore's paradox is the sentence, "it is raining, but I do not believe that it is raining." It is clear that no sane person can say this.

The case of the belief system is different from the case of the bridge in the following way. Holding false beliefs often has no observable consequences. If the bridge is flawed, there is a big, loud crash. But if the belief system is flawed, often there is no crash; it can be a very quiet affair. One simply goes around living in an illusion, without any idea that the images dancing before one's eyes are really phantoms.

Math and science live and die on skepticism. A mathematician will only accept a mathematical proposition as true if it is literally impossible to doubt that proposition without doubting the foundations of mathematics itself. Science refines its theories by the process of looking for any possible flaw in them. A scientist tries to tear their peers' work to shreds; and they are not doing their job if they don't.

Only when we have tested our beliefs in the fires of skepticism, can we be confident that they are true. If everything that you believe is something that you have vigorously doubted, then you will rarely be wrong. Skepticism thus opens up the possibility of a new kind of confidence in our beliefs: the confidence that comes from having survived through terrible difficulty.

It is a most healthy mental habit, when one thinks a thought, to reflexively ask, "but can I find any reasons why that might be wrong?" It would of course be absurd and impossible to do this with every thought. One needs an instinct for doubting at the proper moment. One needs an unconscious reflex, which kicks in without requiring the slightest thought, whenever an idea smells like it needs to be doubted.

Two failure modes for skepticism are *motivated skepticism*, and its opposite, *motivated credulity*. We tend not to look hard for flaws in things that we believe, and we tend to look hard for flaws in things that contradict what we believe. We tend to look hard for flaws in ideas that we don't want to believe, and we tend not to look hard for flaws in ideas that we want to believe.

Skepticism, if it is to do more good than harm, must be applied in a balanced fashion. One must doubt others' ideas and one's own ideas alike. One must doubt attractive ideas and unattractive ideas alike. Failure to apply the principle of balance results in a person who is very good at defending the beliefs that they know and like. They have improved their odds of winning arguments, and they have reduced the frequency with which they have to change their mind, but they have not improved their odds of being right. Their skepticism is a waste of mental effort, at least if their goal is to hold true beliefs and not hold false beliefs.

Besides applying skepticism in an unbalanced fashion, it is also possible to have too little skepticism across the board. There is a type of person who believes everything they hear. This person probably has many false beliefs. The cure is more skepticism.

It is also possible, though much rarer, to have too much skepticism across the board. I had a friend who, for a while, responded to almost every idea by asking, "but what if everything we know is wrong?"

We cannot have absolute certainty about anything. But, there comes a point at which it is no longer useful to doubt. There comes a point at which skepticism serves only to cloud the mind without contributing anything useful.

To this line of thinking one may object, "but it is not intellectually honest to accept something as true without being certain of it. Therefore we should doubt everything of which we are not absolutely certain."

Unfortunately, we cannot have absolute certainty about anything. Past a certain point, skepticism becomes nothing more than being hung up about the fact of our lack of absolute certainty. This is useless and will not lead anywhere. We must accept the impossibility of absolute certainty, and then get on with our lives.

Trust

If we should be skeptical, then the reciprocal principle is that we should not trust. We ought not to take any idea on faith. We ought not to trust ideas that come from outside us, unless they also come from inside us. Rationality is essentially the only mode of inquiring into truth which adopts this principle wholeheartedly.

The principle of not trusting outside sources is part of the seed idea of rationality. Rationality found its roots in the Ancient Greek philosophers. The tradition of Ancient Greek philosophy began with the Milesian naturalists. Seeing the contradictory explanations of natural phenomena according to various gods, they were inspired to reject all of the traditional explanations and do their own inquiries into the nature of things. The Milesian naturalists were the first rationalists; and it is easy to trace the genealogy of our modern science and mathematics back to their initial inspiration. Thus we see that rationality began with the decision not to trust tradition, popular belief, or any other outside source in inquiring into truth.

The beliefs of science and mathematics are not a faith, because one does not need to take them on faith. One does not need to trust anything other than one's own senses and intellect in order to arrive at the beliefs of math and science. There is no authority in rationality; nobody tells anybody else what to believe.

This is possible because for every belief of math and science, any person can see for themselves that it is true. If one doubts a mathematical theorem, one can review the proof and verify its correctness. If one doubts a scientific fact, one can perform the experiments and see what happens.

In contrast, beliefs outside the sphere of rationality are frequently determined by tradition, popular consensus, and appeal to authority. This is generally true, for instance, of religious beliefs.

The first disadvantage of this arrangement is that one cannot check one's facts. If a Catholic doubts a particular claim of the Catholic Church, they have no way to find out for themselves whether or not it is right. In contrast, if a rationalist doubts a claim they read in a scientific journal, they can always check it for themselves.

The second disadvantage of trusting outside sources is that one cannot add new facts to one's belief system. If a Catholic wonders about a question which their faith does not answer, they have no good way to answer it. In contrast, if a rationalist has a question, they know exactly how to go about answering it.

It is as if the Catholic owns a machine which has a proprietary design, whose casing cannot be opened up. If it breaks, they cannot fix it. If it doesn't do something they want it to do, they have no way to make it do so. The rationalist, on the other hand, understands how their machine works. Its design is freely available, and the tools to modify it come in the package. If their machine breaks, they can fix it, and if it doesn't do something they would like it to do, they can modify it so that it does.

The difference is that rationality makes public not only its beliefs, but its methods of arriving at those beliefs. If one merely believes a mathematical or scientific idea, one does not yet understand it. One understands it if one knows not only *what* it says, but also *why* it is true. Then one would believe it even if everybody else changed their minds.

In rationality, one's beliefs come from within oneself as well as from outside oneself. One need not believe anything unless one's own inner voice says that it is true. People agree on mathematical and scientific facts because every person's inner voice says, when they ask it, that these mathematical and scientific facts are true. In every case, we can follow the line of reasoning and see for ourselves that it is so.

No coercion is needed to believe the facts of rationality. If one's inner voice said, for instance, that Cantor's diagonal argument was wrong, then one would be within rationality in attempting to disprove it; and one might even be successful. This sort of thing happens from time to time. The basic reason that there is such a high level of consensus in rationality is simply that people's inner voices tend to say the same things.

We are happy, then, that rationality has provided us with intellectual freedom, and that this freedom has led us to a truth which is not based on faith. But what happens if we give up this freedom by trusting an outside source? We lose the ability to check our beliefs. We lose the ability to show others that our beliefs are correct. We lose the ability to extend our belief system with new information when we desire it. We lose the ability to fix inconsistencies in our beliefs. Moreover, we lose a certain confidence which comes from standing solely on one's own strength. It seems then that it is best not to trust anything spoken by another, unless one's own inner voice speaks it as well.

Evidence

Generally, there are two methods of justifying beliefs: by reasoning, and by evidence. When one justifies a conclusion by reasoning, one begins with some already accepted premises, and shows that the rules of logic imply that the conclusion is true, given that the premises are true. When one justifies a conclusion by evidence, one does this by gathering new facts from observing the world.

Mathematics and philosophy usually advance their conclusions by reasoning alone. Science advances its conclusions by a combination of evidence and reasoning.

Science uses formal, rigorous methods of evidence-gathering to advance its conclusions; but we can apply the principle in a more informal way in our own experience. For instance, suppose I believe that a particular mystical technique is effective. I can ask, what is my evidence for believing this? And does the evidence in fact entail the conclusion?

This evidence will be informal and drawn from my own experience. But in this case — and most cases of importance in ordinary life — I do not have the resources to study the matter rigorously, and it may even be that there is currently no way to study the matter rigorously. So being able to gather, examine and interpret evidence in an informal and unscientific way, while maximizing the fidelity of one's conclusions, is a useful skill.

One of the major failure modes for gathering evidence for one's beliefs is known as *confirmation bias*. Confirmation bias is the fact that we tend to notice evidence that supports our beliefs more than we notice evidence that fails to support our beliefs. This results in the illusion that our beliefs are extensively backed up by the evidence, when in fact this may not be the case. The cure is to make a conscious effort to look for evidence that goes against our beliefs.

Resolving Disagreements

As I pointed out in the section on justification, creating agreement is one of the basic goals of rationality, because it is mainly by creating agreement that we can be confident that our beliefs are true.

We can see, on the social scale, such disagreements as the debate between evolution theory and creationism. In academia, we can see disagreements such as that between Bayesians and frequentists in statistics, or between realists and anti-realists in the philosophy of science. And each of us has experienced, in our own lives, a persistent disagreement with somebody else.

How do we resolve all these persistent disagreements? It can be very hard, and it requires cooperation between the disagreeing parties.

Firstly, it is usually, but not always, the case that in a persistent disagreement, each side is neither completely right nor completely wrong. In these cases, resolving the disagreement requires finding a third option. This involves a significant amount of creativity. It usually requires deeply understanding both sides, and the advantages and problems of both, and then pulling in additional material which nobody in the debate had in mind at all. All of this is then assembled into the third option.

The best starting assumption with a persistent disagreement is that a third option is required. But once we have adopted this as our axiom, we need to avoid falling into the trap of assuming that the right answer is *always* a third option. Sometimes one side really is right, or one side really is wrong. Recognizing these cases can be difficult.

The foregoing material applies when we have come across an already existing debate (e.g., frequentism vs. Bayesianism). We are not personally involved, and our desire is simply to find the truth. If we are personally entangled in a debate — if we *are* one of the two sides — then additional skills are required.

First, we must resist the impulse to prove that we are right and the other wrong. This impulse is a very easy option, psychologically speaking, to take. But, since most persistent disagreements require a third option, it is rarely right. What's more, we may be the ones who are wrong!

In the vast majority of disagreements — and perhaps, in fact, in every disagreement — the two sides do not fully understand each others' positions. The first thing that one should do in a disagreement, before attempting to resolve it, is to attempt to understand and be understood. One should understand not only what the other is claiming, but why they are claiming it. And one should cause the other person to understand the same for oneself — which probably involves introspecting to the point that it is possible to give them this understanding.

If full mutual understanding could be achieved, there would be no disagreement left. If both sides saw all the same information, they could not disagree on what it meant. If they still disagreed, this would only indicate that they were not yet looking at the same information.

So the first step in resolving disagreements is to achieve mutual understanding. Once this is achieved, either it will be clear to both that one side is right and the other wrong; or, both sides will be confused, and it will be possible to begin to seek a third option.

This completes our exposition of the principles of rationality. We have outlined the method of seeking the truth which is practiced in math and science, and which has given rise to our most certain and detailed knowledge about the world. We wish to learn from rationality, and apply it to our inquiries into mysticism.

However, we will find that we run up against fundamental limitations in attempting to do this, and these will require us to modify the usual methods of rationality to arrive at methods more appropriate to our purposes. We will find that rationality is not the final and perfect method of seeking the truth, and that it can be surpassed towards a more complete method.

"There is a meme which says that a certain ritual of cognition is the paragon of reasonableness and so defines what the reasonable people do. But alas, the reasonable people often get their butts handed to them by the unreasonable ones, because the universe isn't always reasonable.

Reason is just a way of doing things, not necessarily the most formidable; it is how professors talk to each other in debate halls, which sometimes works, and sometimes doesn't. If a horde of barbarians attacks the debate hall, the truly prudent and flexible will abandon reasonableness."

- Eliezer Yudkowsky, "Rationality is Systematized Winning"

4

RATIONALITY AND INTUITIONS

CONSIDER the belief, "it is wrong to kill people." Philosophers have attempted, for the past two thousand years, to prove logically that this is true. They have not succeeded. We cannot prove, through reasoning or evidence, that it is wrong to kill people. Nonetheless, we continue to believe this.

This is a rather surprising fact from the perspective of rationality. Rationality tells us that we should justify our beliefs. But, as we have just seen, there are beliefs which we cannot justify, and which we nonetheless feel we ought to go on believing. Does this spell doom for the basic premises of rationality? It seems intuitive this is a case where, as Yudkowsky says, the *reasonable* thing to do is not the thing we in fact ought to do. Let us clarify the problem. Rationality is the proper way of operating in the domain of logic. Thus, it tells us what to believe when, and only when, our beliefs are logical. The belief "it is wrong to kill people," as it happens, is not a strictly logical belief; it mixes logical and experiential concepts.

The word "kill" has a well-defined logical meaning. We can say fairly precisely what it means to kill somebody. Killing plays a part in our reductionist model of the world.

The word "wrong," however, is experiential. We cannot say precisely what it means for something to be wrong. A thousand years of ethics, and a hundred years of meta-ethics, have shown this to be true. The word "wrong" embodies a state of feeling, or an intuitive concept. It is best interpreted experientially, rather than logically.

Thus, the sentence "it is wrong to kill" straddles the boundary between logic and experience, ascribing experiential meaning (wrongness) to something logical (killing).

It should not be extraordinarily surprising that this sentence cannot be justified by the methods of rationality. By being unjustifiable and worth believing, it breaks the rules of rationality. But it breaks the rules of rationality only because it steps outside the domain of rationality.

In the domain of experience, we have ethical intuitions which tell us, in ways that we cannot explain or justify, what is right and what is wrong. These ethical intuitions are what lead us to believe that it is wrong to kill people.

Are there any strictly logical beliefs which we should hold and cannot justify? Ideally, there would not be. However, we will encounter a number of places where it seems that we need to break this standard.

Let us first consider an example from the field of metamathematics. Metamathematics is the field of mathematics which studies mathematics itself. Rather than working with mathematical statements about entities such as numbers, or matrices, or vectors, metamathematics works with mathematical statements about mathematical statements.

One famous meta-mathematical statement is the Gödel sentence. It says, informally, "this statement is not provable." The Gödel sentence is true and not provable. We can see this by the following logic. If it were false, then it would be provable, and therefore true. Since the sentence being false leads to a logical contradiction, the sentence must be true. But its being true implies that it is not provable, since that is the very thing that it states. The same conclusion is advanced in a more rigorous way in the proof of Gödel's incompleteness theorem.

We have so far seen two cases in which we can know a statement to be true, and yet be unable to justify it. These cases are when the statement incorporates experiential concepts, and when it is a clever self-referential paradox.

Another case of true and unjustifiable statements are mathematical axioms. In mathematics, certain statements, called "axioms," are assumed to be true, and every other mathematical statement is proven to follow logically from the axioms. Thus the truth of every mathematical statement is predicated on the truth of the axioms which support it, and the axioms are themselves unproven. The axioms are very basic statements, such as "$n < n + 1$" or "two points make a line."

We have seen that there are things which we should believe, and which we cannot justify. This is troubling for the foundations of rationality. We can also find beliefs that are unjustifiable, and arguably true, in the areas of ethics, politics, philosophy, and the foundations of mathematics, as well as religion, spirituality, and mysticism.

Rationality tells us that evidence and reasoning are the two sources of knowledge which we have. When beliefs are true and unjustifiable, they are not founded on evidence or reasoning; rather, they are founded on our intuitions. Our intuitions tell us that it is wrong to kill people, that two points make a line, and that "this statement is not provable" — though neither evidence nor reasoning can show any of these things to be true.

It seems, then, that nobody actually adheres to the epistemology[1] which says that reasoning and evidence are the only sources of knowledge. We always in practice, base our beliefs on other things as well, and attempting to bring our beliefs into conformity with this epistemology results in absurdity.

There are various solutions to this problem. I choose a solution which is extremely simple, and opens up a whole host of new problems. The solution is to revise our epistemology to admit intuitions as a source of knowledge. Then we have three sources of knowledge: reasoning, evidence, and intuitions. This gives us a way to validate the statements we have examined previously, since in every case our intuitions tell us that these are true.

In a way, this is an obvious step to take. An uneducated person's natural behavior is to trust their intuitions. If a Palaeolithic hunter-gatherer had an intuition that there was a tiger on the other side of the hill, they would think that there probably was a tiger on the other side of the hill.

We do not trust our intuitions due to certain features of our education in rationality. Rationality has developed a bias towards excluding intuitions from its inquiries. In part, this is for legitimate reasons; long experience has taught us that intuitions are often unreliable. In part, I think it is a simple cultural bias.

Moreover, I think it reflects biases that exist in certain people's psychology. Some people are logical; other people are intuitive. An especially logical person will naturally tend to mistrust intuitions; and rationalists who reject intuitions are invariably logical people.

---

[1] An epistemology is a philosophy of knowledge. It explains how we know that our beliefs are true.

Admitting intuition as a source of knowledge solves all of the preceding problems. Intuition is the foundation of the beliefs which we previously identified as unjustifiable. So we say, for instance, that we know through intuition that killing is wrong and that two points make a line. We have answered the question of how we know these things.

Unfortunately, it also opens up many new problems. The knowledge which we get through reasoning and evidence is fairly consistent and reliable; and by increasing the rigor of our inquiries, we know how to make this knowledge close to infallible. This is not true of knowledge we acquire through intuitions.

Different people often have contradictory intuitions on a given topic. Furthermore, one person can have different intuitions on a given topic at different times. Thus we contradict each others' intuitions, and we contradict our own intuitions. Much less of this happens when working with evidence and reasoning; and inconsistencies are always eventually resolved.

Another problem with intuitions is that intuitions are not always shareable; it is not always possible to communicate them to another. Again, there is a contrast with evidence and reasoning. With a certain amount of training in science and math, we can reliably give and receive communication of evidence and reasoning on a given topic. But no such discipline currently exists for intuitions.

This problem, and the problem of contradictory intuitions, result in it often being very difficult to resolve disagreements when intuitions are involved. This, in turn, makes it difficult to know what to believe when we admit intuitions into our epistemology, since creating agreement is one of the main ways that we can come to trust our conclusions.

I do not know of any simple and easy solutions to these problems. The process of seeking truth therefore acquires new challenges when we admit intuitions into it.

Why should we even do this? We have already seen that it offers us a foundation for beliefs which previously had no foundation — killing is wrong, two points make a line, etc. But this is arguably not sufficient reason to take such a radical step. It may seem that it creates more problems than it solves.

The real reason I am interested in taking this step is that it solves certain conflicts between rationality and mysticism which are otherwise very difficult to solve.

In the chapter titled *Logic and Experience*, I said that most of mysticism is in the area of experience, whereas rationality is in the area of logic. Pointing this out is sufficient to solve most conflicts between rationality and mysticism; but there are other conflicts which it does not solve, some of which are very serious and do not go away easily.

These conflicts arise when there is some kind of interaction between the logical and the experiential. We have already seen an example of this in the statement "killing is wrong," where a logical concept ("killing") is related to an experiential concept ("wrongness").

We will examine in detail one class of conflicts between rationality and mysticism which result from an interaction between the logical and the experiential. These conflicts have to do with a class of beliefs called metaphysics, and a belief called materialism. In these conflicts we will find more reasons to adopt the revised epistemology I have proposed, which admits intuitions as a source of knowledge.

Metaphysics

When people speculate about the logical structure of reality, they are doing metaphysics. Metaphysical ideas say how reality is, without offering valid reasoning or evidence. The absence or presence of valid reasoning and evidence is what differentiates between metaphysics and science.

The claim that God exists is metaphysics.[2] The claim that there is life after death is metaphysics. The claim that matter is conscious is metaphysics. The claim that humans have chakras is metaphysics. The claim that every possible world exists is metaphysics. The claim that angels and demons exist is metaphysics. Materialism is metaphysics.

The problem with metaphysical beliefs is that it is impossible to justify them within the usual rational epistemology: i.e., using only reasoning and evidence. If a metaphysical belief were justifiable, then we would cease to call it metaphysics; we would instead call it science. Everybody would accept it as a commonplace fact, and it would lose the air of mystery and allure which always surrounds metaphysical beliefs.

---

2 This is only true, however, if we interpret the statement "God exists" logically, as asserting the existence of a man in the sky that controls the universe. If we interpret "God exists" experientially, as an expression of the wordless truth revealed in mystical experience, then it is not metaphysics.

Metaphysics is in the domain of logic. Hence, the rules of rationality apply to it. If we wish to adhere to the standards of rationality, then we must reject metaphysics. Of course, I recommend the opposite course of action: that we reject the standards of rationality.

This opens up a whole area of research to us, which attempts to uncover metaphysical truths using intuition. The premise is that we can know things about reality directly through our minds, without the use of logic or the use of our senses. The challenge is to figure out what these things are.

Fake Justifications of Metaphysical Ideas

It is a common hobby in certain circles (New Age authors, paranormal enthusiasts, philosophers, Christian apologists, etc.) to attempt to furnish logical or empirical proofs for various metaphysical beliefs. These proofs are never valid.

Examples of fake proofs of metaphysical beliefs are ESP experiments, logical arguments for the existence of God, attempts to refute materialism, New Age texts which reference science in order to advance their conclusions, and a great preponderance of philosophical arguments, including those of famous philosophers such as Aristotle, Berkeley, and Kant.

I would not be surprised if, in the next two hundred years, one or two currently popular metaphysical ideas were proven to be true. But, in that same time, reams of arguments will be published which purport to prove various metaphysical ideas, and do not. So while it is conceivable that any purported proof of a metaphysical idea could be valid, it is not a possibility which we need take very seriously.

These arguments take ideas that are not rational, and dress them up in the clothes of rationality. They claim to be scientific, or to be logically valid, and on the surface they appear to be so. It may require detailed examination, and a subtle understanding of the principles of rationality, to find the reason that the purported proof is not genuine proof. For this reason, such proofs are likely to appear convincing to many people.

It is my opinion that the authors who present these arguments are not attempting to deceive anybody. I think that in most cases, they genuinely believe their claims. They are not trying to be misleading; they are simply confused.

I think that part of why these proofs exist is that people are not always able to distinguish when they are advancing their conclusions using logic alone, and when they are also using intuitions to advance their conclusions. People do not understand rationality, and so they can think that they are following the principles of rationality when in fact they are not.

Materialism

Materialism is a metaphysical belief which stands somewhat in a class of its own. It states that what exists is the physical world known to science: the world consisting of atoms, molecules, stars, rocks, sushi, etc. There is nothing beyond the physical world. There is no God, and there are no souls, angels, demons, chakras, astral planes, auric fields, etc. The only things to know about the world are the things that science can tell us about the world.

The reason that materialism is different from other metaphysical beliefs is that there are actually strong logical reasons to believe in materialism. But before we go into those reasons, let us first get a clearer idea of what materialism is.

What does materialism assert? This is actually somewhat hard to pin down. Firstly, materialism asserts every scientific fact. Secondly, materialism asserts reductionism. Thirdly, and somewhat more subtly, materialism asserts that the world as science currently knows it is approximately equal to the world as it is.

To explain further, it is conceivable that future scientific inquiry could reveal heretofore unknown aspects of reality: other energies, other dimensions, other types of existence. Perhaps some of these could be similar to things which common metaphysical beliefs hold to exist. There could be such things as souls, or angels and demons, or astral planes, or chakras. Or, perhaps we will find existence as it really is to be totally different from anything that any human ever conceived.

Materialism asserts that none of these things will happen. In a rather vague and unspecified way, it asserts that we already have a pretty good idea of what is. The only things that exist are the things currently known to science. We can expect there to be no major surprises in terms of the fundamental makeup of reality.

What reasons do we have to believe in materialism? Materialism asserts every scientific fact, and we have very good reasons to believe in these scientific facts. Materialism asserts reductionism, and, as previously noted, the entire thrust of science is in support of reductionism. These two parts of the belief, then, are quite well-justified — leaving aside the ongoing controversy about reductionism.

What reasons do we have to believe that the world that we know is approximately equal to the world that is? This is a subtler issue. Do we expect future advances in our knowledge to be unsurprising, or do we expect them to be surprising? Exactly how surprised do we expect to be?

Upon formulating the question, we see that it is a little silly. Can we really support a specific vision of what future advances in knowledge will reveal? The future is hard to predict; and this is particularly true at this juncture in history, when the world is changing so quickly. So I doubt that there is a *right answer* to the question of how surprised we ought to expect to be by future discoveries.

This portion of materialism, then, seems to be based not so much on rigorous logical justification, as on aesthetic taste. To some it is very appealing to believe that we know what's going on; and when one has a model as tight and clean as materialism, the appeal is even greater. I have also heard it suggested that the parsimonious manner in which physics explains every known phenomenon makes it unlikely that major revisions will be required to our knowledge of the world.

The Problem

Unfortunately, materialism is, to a great extent, in conflict with mysticism. This constitutes a major problem for the project of reconciling rationality and mysticism. With reductionism we were able to say, "it does not matter for our purposes whether it is true or false." But it seems that we cannot do this with materialism, for reasons which I will now state.

Mysticism holds that one of the principal purposes of life is to achieve progressively greater levels of spiritual development, ultimately resulting in states of being which transcend the suffering of our current condition, and are unimaginably richer and more meaningful.

This belief is already in conflict with materialism, because materialism holds that there is no intrinsic purpose to life; rather, there are only the subjective purposes that humans impose on it. But this is not the most serious conflict.

There is no life after death under materialism. Every part of a human is permanently annihilated when they die. If this is the case, then whatever spiritual development occurs in the course of a person's life will be permanently lost when they die.

A single human lifetime is not long enough to achieve the levels of spiritual development which mysticism holds to be possible. Therefore, in order for this to occur, it must be possible for spiritual development to accumulate over many lifetimes. It must not be the case that every time a person dies, the spiritual development which they achieved during life is permanently lost.

The most obvious way that this could occur would be through reincarnation. There are also other workable hypotheses. For instance, it could be the case that when a person dies, the aspects of their personality are broken up and returned to some global pool, and then re-mixed to create the personalities of new people.

It is clear, at any rate, that this basic premise of mysticism demands some form of life after death in order to be workable. Since there is no life after death under materialism, this premise is incompatible with materialism. But this is not the only conflict between materialism and mysticism.

Another class of conflicts has to do with the mystical optimism about existence. Mysticism involves a feeling of all-embracing love for reality, of the fundamental goodness of existence. This feeling is quite defining for the mystical outlook on life; the mystic feels that their sense of existence's goodness is not merely an attitude, but a revelation of the way things are.

Some mystics believe that badness does not exist. Other mystics believe in badness, but always with the sense that badness is overcome by goodness: that there is an inevitable resolution of all badness in some ultimate goodness. It is fairly clear that this feeling cannot be justified under materialism. Under materialism, goodness is a human concept which bears no relation to the forces that guide the universe. The universe itself is amoral and indifferent.

For the universe to be good, it must be the case that apparent badness resolves itself in a higher goodness. For instance, suffering must serve a higher good. Furthermore, for the universe to be good, it must be the case that humanity contains immense possibilities for goodness which have not yet been actualized — because what humanity has experienced so far does not indicate a good universe. It contains too much suffering, and too little hope.

However, there is no physical law which guarantees a brighter future. There is nothing in the laws of physics which says that suffering always has a purpose. There is no extra term in the equations which forbids the permanent annihilation of a person's personhood when their body dies. There is nothing in the laws of physics which results in anything that humans would consider to be a purpose of existence.

According to materialism, everything is determined by the physical laws. The physical laws allow for a person to suffer and die for no reason, and for no greater good, but just because the math says that they are to suffer and die. The physical laws allow for the possibility that humans on Earth are the only conscious beings in existence, and that in the next ten years we will annihilate ourselves in a nuclear war, or be eaten up by nanotechnology. No tragedy is so great that the laws of physics forbid it. Nothing is so morally reprehensible that physics disallows it. There is no higher truth which consoles us for these injustices. It just is this way; that's how the math works out; there is nothing that helps humans to make emotional sense of it. The universe does not justify itself to us, and it offers no apologies. So goes materialism.

The universe which is described by materialism is not a good universe, and people who believe in materialism commonly have existential issues. I might go so far as to say that anybody who believes in materialism, and does not have existential issues, does not have an entirely realistic perspective on life. I do not think that one can rationally look at the universe which is described by materialism, and be satisfied with it.

The Solution

We have noticed that materialism and mysticism seem to be fundamentally incompatible: firstly, because extended spiritual development is impossible under materialism, and secondly, because materialism is inconsistent with the mystical optimism which feels that the universe is good. My solution to this problem is to reject materialism.

When I say that I reject materialism because it describes a universe that is not good, there is the possibility that one will misinterpret me as meaning that I reject materialism because I do not like it.

The fact that materialism is depressing is not in itself sufficient to imply that materialism is false. There is a distinction between what is true, and what we wish to be true: between "is," and "should." One could argue, therefore, that I have given no reason to reject materialism.

This, however, would be based on a misunderstanding of the nature of the mystical optimism which is in conflict with materialism. This optimism is not a desire for the universe to be good; it is a feeling that the universe *is* good. It feels epistemic, and it has the power to convince its experiencer. It blends "is" and "should" so that no distinction can be drawn between the two.

Now I lapse into the first person. In me, this feeling is so powerful that I find it impossible to suppress. I have repeatedly tried to make myself to stop believing that the universe is good. I have wielded heroic skepticism against this idea. I have employed the most intense efforts, and the cleverest mental gymnastics, in a desperate bid to cause myself to stop thinking this. I have sometimes succeeded temporarily; but always the feeling of optimism has finally won out. So my psychological experiments have yielded the result that I have no choice but to believe that the universe is good. Nor have I succeeded, after similar efforts, in convincing myself that the universe described by materialism is good. The only way I see to resolve the inconsistency is to reject materialism. Let us flesh this line of thinking out in more detail:

i. The universe revolves around some ultimate goodness. This is what is called "God," "brahman," "the Tao," etc. In mystical experience we have glimpses of this goodness.
ii. The purpose of human life is to come closer to this goodness. This is the process of spiritual development. All humans will eventually achieve the greatest possible heights of spiritual development.
iii. Since one lifetime is not long enough to accomplish this, it follows that the process of spiritual development continues beyond the death of the body.
iv. As follows from (iii), a human being is more than their brain and body.

There is nothing surprising about these beliefs; they are common to almost every religious, spiritual, and mystical tradition. (i) and (ii) are founded on intuitions which I and many others find it impossible to reject. (iii) and (iv) are implications of (i) and (ii). The argument is compelling to anybody who accepts the premises. Thus, we reject materialism.

From a rational perspective, this is a rather ugly solution to the problem. It is ugly because we cannot give a proper justification for rejecting materialism. We have no logical reason to reject materialism, and very strong logical reasons to accept it. So we are going against the grain of rationality in a major way by rejecting it. Fortunately, we are not doing so in an unprecedented way; as we noted at the beginning of the chapter, there are a variety of beliefs which we cannot justify, and nonetheless hold.

The belief that the universe is good is not logical, but experiential. It so happens that this is a case, like the sentence "it is wrong to kill," where the logical and the experiential interact. Thus from the experiential belief, "the universe is good," we derive a logical belief, "materialism is false." This, as already stated, goes against the rationalist epistemology.

We cannot make exceptions in our epistemology. If we are to follow an epistemology, we must follow it all the time. So in my case, I was dissatisfied with the preceding resolution for a long time, because it broke the rules of my epistemology. In order to solve the problem genuinely, I had to change my epistemology so that the preceding resolution no longer broke the rules. I did this by admitting intuitions as a source of knowledge.

I find it reasonable to say that the intuitions that come from mystical experience constitute a genuine justification of (i) and (ii). The reason why we cannot *give* a justification for (i) and (ii) is that it is impossible to adequately articulate these intuitions in the form of words. Intuitions are not logical, but experiential; and experiential concepts, unlike logical concepts, cannot reliably and in every case be put into words. Thus, it seems that we obtain a situation where we are perfectly justified in holding these beliefs, only we cannot say what our justification is.

This situation creates problems both for the mystic and for the non-mystic. The problem for the mystic is that they cannot justify themselves to others. The problem for the non-mystic is that they cannot know whether or not they should take the mystic seriously.

I have spent a great deal of time discussing my position with convinced materialists. These conversations, though perfectly civil, always end in an impasse. The basic problem is that I understand their position, but they do not understand mine. I have a very solid grasp on what materialism is and why people believe it. However, I have never met a convinced materialist who understood mystical intuitions.

Both the materialist position, and the mystic position, have much in their favor. In rejecting materialism, we are rejecting a position which has an awful lot going for it. If we reject it in a full understanding of what it has going for it, then what we are saying is simply that the other side has more going for it. When we place them on the scale, the scale tips to one side rather than the other. The materialist often thinks that I do not feel the weight that their position has; but I do. It is simply that I feel more weight from the other side. The materialist does not feel the pull of that particular weight, and so they find it hard to believe that it could in fact be heavier.

Let us now review the line of thinking we have followed. People sometimes believe things that they cannot justify through evidence and reasoning. This means that we cannot accept the epistemology which says that knowledge comes only from evidence and reasoning. We can resolve this problem by revising our epistemology to admit intuitions as a third source of knowledge.

This revision makes it possible for us to begin to study "metaphysics:" that is, the inquiry into the nature of reality beyond what is known to science. As the first step of this project, it also allows us to reject materialism. This is desirable because materialism conflicts with two important mystical intuitions. The first intuition is that the purpose of life is to achieve spiritual development, and that every person will eventually reach the greatest heights of spiritual development. This is impossible under materialism because it requires life after death. The second intuition is that the universe is good, which is incompatible with materialism because the universe described by materialism is not good. These points offer us compelling reasons to reject materialism. We can justify this rejection by admitting intuitions as a source of knowledge. We simply acknowledge the intuitions that would lead us to reject materialism as having epistemic weight.

Admitting intuitions as a source of knowledge turns out to be very useful for mystical thinking in general. It opens up countless new lines of interesting research. So the conflict between mysticism and materialism is by no means the only good reason to make this revision.

"The archetypical mind is intended to heighten this ability to express the Creator in patterns more like the fanned peacock's tail, each facet of the Creator vivid, upright, and shining with articulated beauty."

- Ra, The Law of One

5

ARCHETYPES

BEFORE taking the next step, let us look back and review what has been accomplished so far. I have spent the past three chapters laying the foundations of my proposed approach to seeking the truth. I began with the distinction between logic and experience. On this basis I presented my basic strategy for reconciling rationality and mysticism, which is the rejection of logical interpretations of mystical ideas. Then I discussed the basic principles of rationality. Next I recommended that we admit intuitions as a source of knowledge, and pointed out various philosophical problems that are solved by doing this.

Now we are ready to study mystical thinking in a more direct way. It has been my experience that mystical thinking, like poetry or literature, follows definite patterns. And so, it is possible to study mystical thoughts from an analytic perspective which seeks to extract these patterns and thus understand the thoughts from within a more general framework. In this chapter we develop such a framework. The framework centers around the concept of "archetypes."

Some readers may find that this chapter departs from the clear, understandable style of the preceding chapters. This is somewhat unavoidable, due to the inherent difficulty of explaining mystical concepts within the language of philosophy.

It is a task a bit like trying to write a Martian to English dictionary. I apologize if it seems to the reader that I have not successfully bridged the gap.

Types of Mystical Thinking

It will be useful to consider mystical thinking as dividing into two types: practical, and theoretical. Practical mystical thinking gives us advice on how to live our lives, telling us what to do and how to do it. Theoretical mystical thinking tells us about the nature of reality. Theoretical mystical thinking is concerned with the "is," and practical mystical thinking is concerned with the "should." The division is somewhat artificial, because generally in mystical texts these two types of thinking are freely intermingled. The "is" and the "should" are laid down in the same breath. But the division will nonetheless prove useful for us.

Practical mystical thinking cannot be, and does not need to be, evaluated on a strictly rational basis. The prevailing confusion in the fields of ethics and meta-ethics indicates that we do not have sound logical justifications for what we think we should do. No sound argument exists to the effect that we should not kill each other; but we nonetheless believe that we should not. So principles of how to live one's life appear to fall outside the sphere of what rationality can strictly determine for us.

Theoretical mystical thinking thus forms the main sticking point in terms of synthesizing rationality and mysticism. Rationality and theoretical mystical thinking are in gross conflict with each other, because theoretical mystical thinking hardly ever adheres to rational principles, but it sometimes seems like it should.

In attempting to address this conflict, I arrived at a division of theoretical mystical thinking into two non-exhaustive categories. These categories are metaphysics and archetypal thinking. Metaphysics was discussed in the chapter titled *Rationality and Intuitions* and archetypal thinking is the subject of this chapter.

At this point we may take a moment to draw a diagram (Fig. 1) of all of the different pieces into which we have now analyzed the concept *mysticism*:

In terms of synthesizing rationality and mysticism, the division between metaphysics and archetypal thinking is useful because each of these types of thinking has a different relationship to rationality. Since metaphysics is a logical discipline, it strongly seems like it ought to follow the rules of rationality. So reconciling it with rationality requires taking the radical step of admitting intuitions as a source of knowledge. On the other hand, archetypal thinking

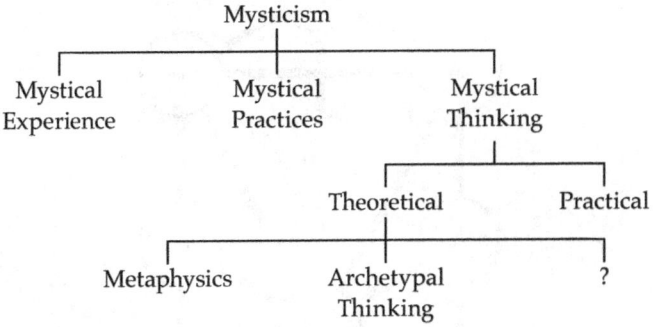

Fig. 1: An Analysis of the Concept 'Mysticism'

is mostly experiential, and so reconciling it with rationality is much simpler. We only have to point out that it is an experiential discipline rather than a logical one, and therefore has nothing to do with rationality.

Archetypes

Archetypal thinking works with a particular type of concept called an *archetype*. What is an archetype? How do we distinguish archetypes from concepts that are not archetypes?

An archetype is an abstract facet of human experience. Examples of archetypes are happiness, logic, femininity, evil, heroism, submissiveness, humor, love, sensation, conflict, passivity, power, beauty, fear, modesty, patience, and creativity.

Additionally, the component concepts of *systems of archetypes* — to be covered in detail later in the section of the same title — are archetypes. Systems of archetypes include the Tree of Life (Fig. 2), the Tarot (Fig. 3), the twelve astrological signs (Fig. 4), the four elements (Fig. 5), the seven chakras (Fig. 6), the Enneagram (Fig. 7), and the taijitu (Fig 8).

The meta-theory of archetypal thinking, in the precise form which I present here, is my own invention. But, the activity which it describes is not. What I call archetypal thinking has been practiced

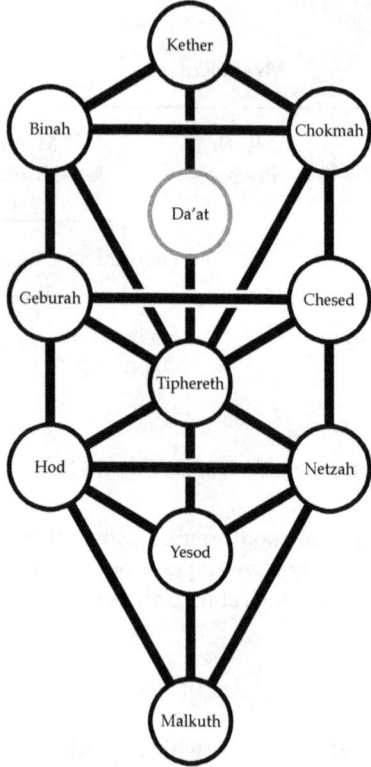

Fig. 2: The Kabbalah Tree of Life

In Judaic mysticism, the tree of life is an important integral part of the Kabbalah. It takes the form of an interconnected mesh of ten nodes, representing the ten Sephiroth or ten emanations and attributes of God that sustain the universe.

Other interpretations of the tree life exist and are distinguished by their spelling – i.e. the Christian Cabbala and the Hermetic Qabalah. In the Hermetic interpretation, a hidden sephiroth, Da'at, is added to represent knowledge and is considered to be part of Binah.

The relationship between the soul of man and the Divine, gives Kabbalah one of its two central metaphors in describing Divinity, the other being the Ohr (light) metaphor. Kabbalah repeatedly stresses the need to avoid all corporeal interpretation and through this, the sephiroth related to the structure of the body are reformed into Personas. Underlying the structural purpose of each sephiroth is a hidden motivational force which is understood best by comparison with a corresponding psychological state in human spiritual experience. Therefore, the sephiroth describe the spiritual life of man, and constitute the conceptual paradigm in Kabbalah for understanding everything.

Fig. 3: The Tarot

The tarot is a deck of cards, usually numbering 78, that was used from the mid-15th century in Europe to play a group of popular card games such as French tarot or Italian tarocchini. It was only from the late 18th century that their use was turned towards mysticism as a map for spiritual pathways or as a method of divination.

In 1871, swiss clergyman Antoine Court de Gébelin, published Le Monde Primitif, a speculative study of the survival of religious symbolism in the world at that time. It was he who first asserted that the symbolism within the Tarot de Marseille represented the secrets of the mysteries associated to Isis and Thoth. He further claimed that the word 'Tarot' was a fusion of the Egyptian words tar, meaning 'royal' and ro, meaning road, so that the word tarot should be synonymous with the 'royal road' to wisdom.

Unfortunately, these claims were made before Jean-François Champollion had deciphered Egyptian hieroglyphs or before the Rosetta Stone had even been discovered. Since this claim, Egyptologists have not found anything in the ancient Egyptian language to support Gébelin's extravagant claims. Despite this, the identification of the tarot cards with the Egyptian Book of Thoth was already firmly established in occult practice and continues in modern urban legend to the present day..

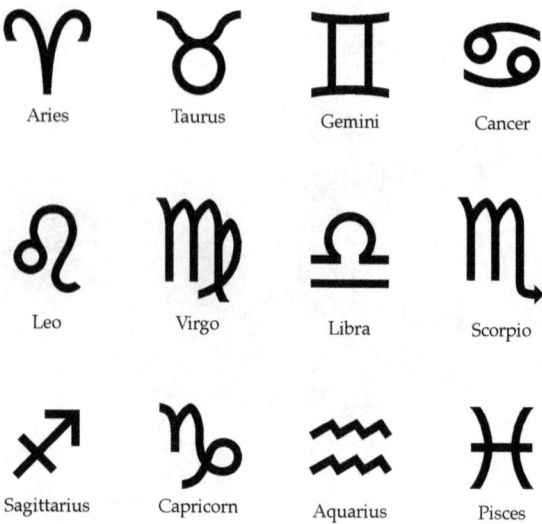

Fig. 4: The Twelve Astrological Signs

The astrological signs of the zodiac represent the division of the ecliptic plane into twelve equal segments, each represented by its dominant constellation. Modern astrology is based on that of the Babylonians and Greeks, but other systems still exist, notably those of China and India.

Ancient observers of the heavens developed elaborate systems of explanation for divination, based on the movements of the sun, moon, and planets through the constellations of the zodiac. At some point, the influences of these planetary bodies were ascribed to certain characteristics and tendencies and then associated with a person's time and place of birth.

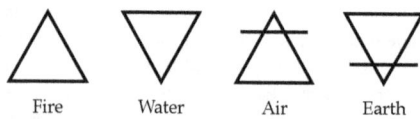

Fig. 5: The Four Elements

The four elements can be found in many cultures and esoteric practices. They are used exoterically to describe the four states of matter and esoterically to represent the qualities of those states, such as water representing the nature of mind. The symbols shown here are from Alchemy but they are also portrayed in other forms. For example, in astral projection techniques, a square is used to represent the element Earth whilst at the base of a Buddhist stupa, a cube is used. The four elements are usually associated with a fifth element, representing spirit.

Fig. 6: The Seven Chakras

The word chakra is sanskrit for 'wheel' or 'turning'. It is a concept that originates in ancient Hindu texts, such as the Upanishads and features in yogic and tantric traditions of Hinduism and Buddhism. The concept itself refers to wheel-like vortices of subtle energy that occur at specific points within the human body, possibly at the interconnections of subtle energy channels. Differing spiritual philosophies posit a varying number of chakras, including a division of major and minor. In the West, the seven chakra system has now become the most widely adopted. During the 1940s, this approach was adapted to associate a given colour from the visible spectrum to each of the seven chakras -- a move which bears no relevance to the original concept.

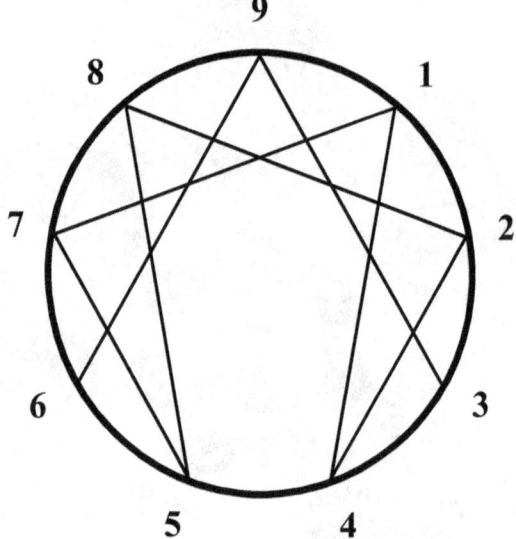

Fig. 7: The Enneagram

The enneagram is a nine-pointed figure associated with the Fourth Way teachings of G.I. Gurdjieff. It is a term derived from two greek words, ennea (nine) and grammos (something drawn or written down).

It was first openly published in 1947 in P.D. Ouspensky's book, In search of the Miraculous. Within chapter 14, Ouspensky provides details of a lecture given by Gurdijeff about its meaning.

Within the circle, a triangle connects the points 9, 3 and 6, whilst the inscribed figure connects the other points in a cycle of 1, 4, 2, 8, 5 and 7. The derived number corresponds to the recurring decimal .142857 which is 1/7th. These six points together with the point numbered 9 are said to relate to the notes of a musical octave and therefore represent the main stages of any complete process. The points 3 and 6 are said to represent "shock points" or catalytic events that affect how a process develops.

The provenance of the enneagram has also been linked with Sufism and the Jewish Kabbalah Tree of Life.

Fig. 8: The Taijitu

There are many varieties of Taijitu symbols in use but this version has become the most widely known. It is named after the Confucian philosopher Zhou Dunying from the Song dynasty 960-1279C.E. and depicts two fish-like figures inside a circle.

The white side of the symbol represents movement or "greater yang" whilst the black side of the symbol represents stillness or "greater yin". Within each side of the symbol is a small circle of the opposite colour signifying the principle that each side arises from its complementary opposite. This principle also includes the idea of balance between the two forces of stillness and movement, with a certainty that when the each side reaches its maximum, it will give birth to its opposite.

The concept of Yin and Yang is a fundamental theory within the Chinese worldview. Seen as a pair of interacting opposites, Yin and Yang is a way and means of understanding the nature and composition of everything within the universe. Yang is seen as an active or creative state, often associated with masculinity whilst Yin is seen as a passive or receptive state, often associated with femininity. However, whether a thing is considered Yin or Yang is not down to its inherent property. Rather, a thing is considered Yin or Yang according to the role it plays in relation to other things. Therefore, Yin and Yang are a dynamic principle, in which each becomes dominant and receptive in turn.

for the entirety of recorded history. There have also been previous attempts to describe the practice systematically, as I do here. Plato's *Theory of Forms* is an example of such an attempt.

Let us attempt to clarify further what an archetype is. Archetypes have the following characteristics:

1. *Human universality*. Every human[1] comes into contact with every archetype at some point or in some way. Archetypes are not time-bound or culture-bound, though a particular representation of an archetype may be so bound. For instance, the Roman goddess Venus is an archetype, and culture-bound. But everything that Venus *means* is a human universal; it is only the particular representation and arrangement of archetypal material which is culture-bound.

2. *Experienceability*. An archetype is a quality which can be directly experienced. An archetype is subjective, not objective. If "strawberry" were an archetype, then the archetype would be the taste of strawberries or the sight of strawberries, and not strawberries themselves.

3. *Abstraction*. An archetype is general, not specific. It is abstract, not concrete. Thus, even though "defecation" is an universal human experience, it is not an archetype, because it is concrete and not abstract. Similarly, "sex" is not an archetype, but "sexuality" is.

4. *Pervasiveness*. An archetype shows up in a variety of different situations. More pervasive archetypes are more truly archetypes. Thus, "passivity" is more truly an archetype than "modesty."

5. *Resistance to logical analysis*. It is impossible for us to give a logical, reductionist account of an archetype. What does the word "happiness" mean? We cannot say precisely. We know that "happiness" means something, but we do not have the words to explain any further. An archetype is thus, for us, an irreducible thing-in-itself, which we cannot analyze into component parts.

One can tell whether or not a concept is an archetype by the following test. For any archetype, it should be possible for any person, on sufficient reflection, to think of a large number of emotionally charged situations in their past which embodied that archetype. For every archetype, every person will have a litany of associated stories.

---

[1] Every normal human, that is; likely exceptions are feral children or children who die very young.

On the other hand, this should not be true for concepts that are not archetypes; for non-archetypal concepts, there will be no litany of stories.

An archetype, then, is both a domain of experience, and the concept which is the key to that domain of experience. We have a word, such as "pain," which is the key — and then the range of experience which is what it means. The concept itself — the key — is a logical concept which may be manipulated by the logical faculties, and put into relation with other logical concepts. The domain of experience — the meaning — is experiential. Archetypal thinking thus straddles the boundary between logic and experience.

The concept "archetype" is a fuzzy one. There is no sharp dividing line between "archetypes" and "non-archetypes." Thus, for some concepts, the question "is it an archetype?" will simply have no answer.

Is "hotness" an archetype? Is "redness" an archetype? In my opinion, these two concepts lie in the fuzzy region between archetypes and non-archetypes, so that there is no answer to the question of whether or not they are archetypes.

Knowledge of Archetypes

There are three types of knowledge of archetypes. The first type is *knowledge of an individual archetype*. This takes the form of an experiential, intuitive apprehension of the archetype. The more vivid and powerful this apprehension is, the more thoroughly one can be said to know the archetype. No distinction can be made between knowing an archetype and experiencing an archetype.

The second type of knowledge is *knowledge of archetypal significations*. Things and events in the world can signify archetypes. To signify an archetype is to evoke it subjectively. Knowledge of archetypal significations consists of noticing such significations.

An obvious example of signifying is when one uses a word to refer to an archetype. The word "happiness" signifies happiness. Another example of signifying is that of art. A work of art generally signifies an elaborate complex of archetypes.

Experiences also signify archetypes — one can also say that they "embody" archetypes. For instance, when one is one relaxing on the beach with one's lover, perhaps this experience embodies happiness. As previously stated, for every archetype, every person will have a long litany of meaningful experiences which embodied that archetype.

Knowledge of archetypal significations consists of noticing that something signifies an archetype. Sometimes this is very trivial; for instance, it does not take much intelligence to notice that stubbing one's toe signifies pain. Other times it is extremely subtle; for instance, it may take a great deal of intelligence to notice that self-doubt signifies blockage of the third eye chakra, and to identify exactly when one is doubting oneself.

The third type of knowledge of archetypes is *knowledge of the relations between archetypes*.

Relations Between Archetypes

Archetypes stand in definite relations to each other. I am aware of three such classes of relations:

1. *Similarity*. Two archetypes can be similar. "Joy" and "happiness" are similar. "Truth" and "honesty" are similar. "Yang" and "chokhmah" are similar. "Peace" and "death" are similar.

There can also be a relation of equality, or congruence, between archetypes. However, I have found that the equals sign is very easy to abuse in the study of archetypes. It seems to me that to postulate equality between two archetypes is often to lose information about both, by turning each into a box into which the other is then jammed. It often confuses the issue, rather than simplifying it.

One never comes across quite the same archetype twice. Even two experiences of what is ostensibly one archetype will really be somewhat different.

The advantage of the equals sign is that it can simplify thinking about archetypes. When one wishes to ignore details and pay attention to generalities, the use of the equals sign is justified. Systems of archetypes contain many concepts which have clear analogies across systems (such as the Yang-Chokhmah similarity noted earlier). Here the equals sign can be useful, if used wisely.

2. *Opposition*. Two archetypes can be opposites. "Happiness" and "sadness" are opposites. "Light" and "dark" are opposites. "Right" and "wrong" are opposites. "Male" and "female" are opposites. "Love" and "fear" are opposites. "Thinking" and "feeling" are opposites. A pair of opposites can be called a *duality*.

Archetypes very often have opposites. Perhaps every archetype has an opposite. Often an archetype can be said to have more that one opposite. For instance "fear" can be said to be the opposite of love, but "indifference" can also be said to be the opposite of "love."

If one were not thinking sufficiently carefully, one could imagine that the two relations "similarity" and "opposition" together cover all conceivable relations between archetypes. This is not true; archetypes can also be randomly askew to each other, dissimilar but not opposite.

I do not call "randomly askew" a relation between archetypes, because it is uninteresting. It is the relation that most archetypes have to each other. Therefore, I regard it not as a relation, but as the lack of any relation.

3. *Inclusion*. One archetype can include another. "Emotion" includes "happiness." "Love" includes "forgiveness." "Sensation" includes "pleasure." The relation is analogous to the subset relation in set theory.

This third relation, inclusion, seems to me less common and less important than similarity and opposition. However, it does seem to exist. It allows us to identify some archetypes as more general, and others as more specific. We can then say that the more general archetypes are more truly archetypal than the specific archetypes.

The Mystical

The mystical is that which is experienced in mystical experience. The mystical is an archetype. It has a unique position among archetypes as the central and all-encompassing archetype. The mystical includes every archetype within itself.

The mystical is, unsurprisingly, a frequent topic of discussion in mystical texts. We can identify "the Tao," "brahman," the Buddhist "emptiness," etc., as all being archetypes equal to the mystical. In addition, the word "God" means, in some interpretations, the mystical. The mystical is the ultimate goodness postulated in the chapter titled *Rationality and Intuitions*.

That the mystical includes every archetype within itself, implies that the mystical includes all dualities within itself. Thus the mystical includes light and dark, happiness and sadness, right and wrong, etc.

This is connected with the philosophical thesis of *non-dualism*. Non-dualism states, in part, precisely what I have just stated: that the nature of the mystical is non-dual, and it contains all opposites within itself. Non-dualism is also a metaphysical thesis, stating that the mystical is the only thing that exists.

The Relativity of Archetypal Judgments

I argued in the chapter titled *Rationality* that truth is not relative. The saying that "truth is relative," however, is true with respect to archetypal thinking.

Let us return to the three types of knowledge of archetypes. These are knowledge of individual archetypes, knowledge of archetypal significations, and knowledge of the relations between archetypes.

Knowledge of individual archetypes cannot be said to be true or false. It simply is. What can be said to be true or false in the feeling of love, or the feeling of injustice? They are not true or false; they are.

That said, knowledge of individual archetypes is relative to a particular person, moment, and culture. Each person has their own perception of the archetype "love." In each individual instance that a person apprehends love, they have a different perception of the archetype. Furthermore, probably each cultural context has its own particular perception of love. So knowledge of individual archetypes is relative.

Knowledge of archetypal significations is relative. A thing may mean different things to different people. Perhaps an event which appears tragic to one person appears joyous to another.

Knowledge of the relations between archetypes is also relative. If I say that "love is the opposite of fear," it is certainly possible for people to disagree with me in this judgment. Is there a true or false of the matter?

To answer this question, we must ask, what does my statement mean? It will be recalled that the meaning of the statement is experiential. Thus, the only way that I can properly interpret the statement is to gain some kind of intuitive apprehension of the opposition of love and fear. Either I will gain such an apprehension, or I will not gain such an apprehension.

There is, therefore, not so much a question of true or false, as a question of meaningful or meaningless. Does the statement ring with subjective truth, or does it fail to do so? This is "true" or "false" with knowledge of the relations between archetypes; and it is relative to the individual, moment, and culture.

Systems of Archetypes

One of the most interesting applications of archetypes is the study of *systems of archetypes*. A system of archetypes is a fixed set of archetypes which stand in definite relations to each other. As previously stated, examples of systems of archetypes are the Tree of Life (Fig. 2), the Tarot (Fig. 3), the twelve astrological signs (Fig. 4), the four elements (Fig. 5), the seven chakras (Fig. 6), the Enneagram (Fig. 7), and the taijitu (Fig 8).

Consider, by way of example, the Tree of Life from the Judaic Kabbalah (Fig. 2). This system consists of ten archetypes, which are called "Sephiroth." They bear numerous relationships to each other. In particular, it is worth noting the dualities in this system. These are Chokmah/Binah, Chesed/Geburah, and Netzach/Hod.

There are strong metaphysical elements to most interpretations of the Tree of Life. This illustrates the fact that archetypal thinking and metaphysics are, in mystical thinking, almost always freely intermingled.

To study a system of archetypes is to meditate upon the meanings of its constituent archetypes, and to observe how these archetypes show up in one's life. It also usually involves drawing relations between the constituent archetypes, and other archetypes not belonging to the system.

The study of systems of archetypes is bread and butter for mystical thinking. The benefit of systems of archetypes is that they allow one to analyze aspects of one's life, largely having to do with human psychology and spirituality, in a systematic way. A system of archetypes, well-studied, is an extremely parsimonious system which explains a tremendous variety of phenomena. The understanding that one gains from studying the system can have great pragmatic value for mysticism, and for life in general.

One of the interesting things about systems of archetypes is the fact that many different systems of archetypes have significant explanatory power. One can look at the same set of phenomena according to different systems and derive meaningful observations in every case. We are led to ask, therefore: to what extent are the systems of archetypes non-arbitrary? Could I make up my own system of archetypes, and derive just as much meaning from this as I could from using an established system such as the Tarot or the seven chakras?

My experience suggests to me that systems of archetypes are non-arbitrary. They are not completely and rigorously determined, such that any deviation would result in incorrectness, as is the case with scientific theories. But it seems that they are not on the opposite extreme, either; that they are not arbitrary.

Different systems of archetypes yield different levels of explanatory power upon extended study. Some prove extraordinarily meaningful; others prove less meaningful. If all systems of archetypes were equal, one would expect this not to be the case; one would expect the level of meaning yielded to be dependent only on the amount of energy spent in studying the system. But this is not what happens. So the meaning seems not to be contained only in one's attempts to organize one's experience according to a system; it is also contained in the specific system used.

Could one invent one's own system of archetypes, and give it as much explanatory power as systems such as the Tree of Life or the seven chakras? If I were to take a guess at this question, I would say that one could do this; but only in the sense that one could write a piece of music as good as Beethoven's Ninth Symphony, or a play as good as Romeo and Juliet. I guess, in other words, that it is possible in theory; but that it would require a level of genius exceeding almost anybody's capabilities.

Archetypes and Rationality

Is archetypal thinking compatible with rationality? Here we must answer in the affirmative; but only by virtue of the fact that the two hardly enter into any relation with each other.

Archetypal thinking is not a rational process. Archetypal statements do not have any logical meaning, and cannot be confirmed or denied by rational processes. They are so entirely in a different sphere that the question "is archetypal thinking compatible with rationality?" seems absurd. It is akin to the question, "is oil painting compatible with rationality?"

Archetypal thinking, however, does have logical components. An archetypal concept — the key to the storehouse, the word "pain" as opposed to pain itself — is a logical entity. We might think, therefore, that we would have to play by the rules of rationality in studying archetypes.

It seems to me, however, that we do not. Part of archetypal thinking is logical, but archetypal thinking nonetheless has nothing to do with rationality. Their concerns do not overlap. It is as if they are two different games that are played on the same field.

Metaphysics and Archetypal Thinking

As previously stated, much of mystical thinking can be classified as either metaphysics or archetypal thinking. What is the relationship between these two types of thinking?

Metaphysics is a logical discipline, which adds to our logical picture of the world. For instance, with the metaphysical idea of heaven and hell, we take the picture of the world as we know it, and draw over it a world full of clouds and winged creatures, and draw below it a world full of fire and horned creatures. We modify the picture of the world by adding to it propositions about heaven and hell, which are no different from the propositions about aeroplanes and benzene molecules.

Archetypal thinking is a discipline which involves logical concepts, but which is primarily experiential. It deals with logical concepts which are keys to experiential domains of meaning. The logical concepts are simplistic signifiers which are never assembled into complex structures. The substance of archetypal thinking lies in the domain of experience.

Often, a single statement can be interpreted either metaphysically or archetypally. Consider for example the statement, "I tell you the truth, whoever hears my word and believes him who sent me has eternal life and will not be condemned; he has crossed over from death to life."

Interpreted logically, this statement contains metaphysics. Whoever receives Jesus' teachings and believes in God will live forever in heaven.

Interpreted experientially, this statement contains archetypal thinking. "Life" and "eternal life" refer to one archetype. "Death" and "condemnation" refer to another archetype. "Him who sent me" is another archetype. This juxtaposition of archetypes evokes a certain emotional response, and this is the total meaning of the statement.

In mystical thinking, metaphysics and archetypal thinking are rarely distinct. In most cases they are freely intermingled. The distinction between metaphysics and archetypal thinking is an interpretation applied, after the fact, to already existing thoughts.

Archetypes are the mathematics of consciousness. They are the unifying framework within which we may study the psychological and spiritual aspects of our existence. As with mathematics, the study of archetypes is inexhaustible. There is no absolute frame of reference, and there is no set of archetypes which can account for all others.

The kind of knowledge which one can get from studying archetypes is different from the kind of knowledge one can get from rationality. Rational knowledge is logical, whereas archetypal knowledge is logical/experimental.

Whereas rational concepts are precise and rigid, archetypal concepts are fluid, flexible, and fuzzy at the edges. This means that archetypal knowledge is not precise, provable, or unbiased. However, it is useful because it can dynamically account for much more complex systems than rational knowledge can.

Rationality has not been able to penetrate the problem of human psychology, because its requirement for precision and inflexible perfection means that its concepts cannot go far enough to take in such a vast territory. So archetypal thinking constitutes a more powerful mode of thought.

"They exhaust the possibilities of poetry to declare what is demonstrably untrue. For example, we find in the Shiva Sanhita that 'he who daily contemplates on this lotus of the heart is eagerly desired by the daughters of Gods, has clairaudience, clairvoyance, and can walk on the air.' Another person 'can make gold, discover medicine for disease, and see hidden treatures.'

All this is filth. What is the curse upon religion that its tenets must always be associated with every kind of extravagance and falsehood?"

- Aleister Crowley, Liber ABA

6

MYSTICAL THINKING

THE groundwork is now laid for our approach to synthesizing rationality and mysticism. The tools are in place and all that remains is to show you how the tools are used.

In this chapter, we will take mystical texts, and interpret them according to the framework we have laid out. We will say what they mean, what ideas are to be accepted, and what ideas are to be rejected. Hopefully this process will shed light not only on the texts, but on the framework as well.

I hope to demonstrate that mystical ideas, as they exist in practice, can generally be analyzed by these methods, and that in doing so we separate sense from nonsense.

Before beginning, we have one more tool to lay down. It will tell us how to interpret the mystical texts which we are about to consider.

The principle of charitability.

When we can produce multiple interpretations of a statement, and some of these interpretations are true or meaningful whereas others are false or meaningless, then we should assume that it is the true or meaningful interpretations that were meant.

Most frequently this principle will manifest in the following way. We are confronted with a statement which, when interpreted logically, produces a false or meaningless interpretation. The same statement, when interpreted experientially, produces a true or meaningful interpretation. In these cases we will assume the experiential interpretation, rather than the logical interpretation.

Now we begin with the texts:

MUNDAKA UPANISHAD
FIRST MUNDAKA
FIRST KHANDA[1]

1. Brahma was the first of the Devas, the preserver of the world. He told the knowledge of Brahman, the foundation of all knowledge, to his eldest son Atharva.

2. Whatever Brahma told Atharvan, that knowledge of Brahman Atharvan formerly told to Aṅgir; he told it to Satyavâha Bhâradvâga, and Bhâradvâga told it in succession to Aṅgiras.

3. Saunaka, the great householder, approached Aṅgiras respectfully and asked: 'Sir, what is that through which, if it is known, everything else becomes known?'

4. He said to him: 'Two kinds of knowledge must be known, this is what all who know Brahman tell us, the higher and the lower knowledge.'

5. 'The lower knowledge is the Rig-veda, Yagur-veda, Sâma-veda, Atharva-veda, Sikshâ (phonetics), Kalpa (ceremonial), Vyâkarana (grammar), Nirukta (etymology), Khandas (metre), Gyotisha (astronomy); but the higher knowledge is that by which the Indestructible (Brahman) is apprehended.'

6. 'That which cannot be seen, nor seized, which has no family and no caste, no eyes nor ears, no hands nor feet, the eternal, the omnipresent (all-pervading), infinitesimal, that which is imperishable, that it is which the wise regard as the source of all beings.'

7. 'As the spider sends forth and draws in its thread, as plants grow on the earth, as from every man hairs spring forth on the head and the body, thus does everything arise here from the Indestructible.'

8. 'The Brahman swells by means of brooding (penance); hence is produced matter (food); from matter breath, mind, the true, the worlds (seven), and from the works (performed by men in the worlds), the immortal (the eternal effects, rewards, and punishments of works).'

9. 'From him who perceives all and who knows all, whose brooding (penance) consists of knowledge, from him (the highest Brahman) is born that Brahman, name, form, and matter (food).'

---

1 Müller, Max. *The Sacred Books of the East*, vol. 15. Oxford: Oxford University Press, 1884.

Analysis — Mundaka Upanishad, First Khanda

Line 1 references the Hindu god Brahma, who has the epithet "the preserver." Lines 1 to 3 describe a story of how the knowledge contained in this passage was transmitted. These lines are probably best interpreted as mythical, and therefore false.

"Brahman" is a Hindu philosophical concept, distinct from the god Brahma. Brahman is described as the infinite, eternal essence of reality. We can make sense of the concept of Brahman if we equate it with the mystical. Otherwise, it is metaphysics.

The distinction between "lower knowledge" and "higher knowledge," given in lines 4 and 5, is a meaningful one. The phrase "lower knowledge" can be taken as encompassing everything that we would typically call knowledge. The writer gives a list of specific documents comprising "lower knowledge," but we can re-contextualize the idea by equating "lower knowledge" with science, mathematics, and the humanities. "Higher knowledge" is the apprehension of the mystical.

An implication in the naming of these concepts as "higher" and "lower" is that the apprehension of the mystical is more valuable than knowledge such as science, mathematics, and the humanities. Mystics would generally agree with this claim.

Finally, we may ask whether or not the apprehension of the mystical is rightly called "knowledge." I would consider this to be a mistaken question, on the grounds that it is generally considered unwise to hold debates where the only thing under debate is the definition of a word.

Line 6 attempts to describe the nature of Brahman. Phrases such as "omnipresent," "infinitesimal," and "imperishable" are best interpreted experientially.

The same is true of the phrase "which the wise regard as the source of all beings," and the continuation of the idea in line 7. It is a ubiquitous metaphysical idea that the mystical is the source of all things. We cannot know whether or not this is the case, due to our inadequate lack of knowledge to untangle the mystery of the origins of existence. So we reject the metaphysical idea.

If we interpret this phrase experientially, however, then we can derive meaning from this claim, by imagining everything emerging and coalescing out of the mystical, like clay being sculpted, which is a perfectly natural thing to imagine, due to the way that the mystical seems to contain everything. The fact that imagining this is so natural may be related to the fact that the metaphysical idea of the mystical as the origin of existence is so common.

In lines 8 and 9 we have some curious claims. The Brahman is claimed to undergo a mysterious process called "brooding" or "penance," producing in series a number of different aspects of existence. Here it seems that Brahman is to be understood in the metaphysical sense, as the mysterious origin of existence.

It is a common activity in metaphysics to enumerate the substances or categories of existing things, often in the form of a hierarchy or a progression from first to last. This is what is being done here. The specific list is a rather odd one.

In line 9 it appears that the writer is claiming that the mystic is responsible for continuing this process of creation, originating his own list of things and substances. This makes little sense to me.

The writer describes the mystic as "him who perceives all and knows all, whose brooding (penance) consists of knowledge." We can experientially understand the claim that the mystic perceives all and knows all by referring to the fact that the mystical seems to contain everything.

"Knowledge" is presumably to be taken as the combination of "lower knowledge" and "higher knowledge." It is tautological to say that the mystic occupies himself with "higher knowledge." The claim that the mystic also occupies himself with "lower knowledge" is presumably a judgment about the kind of thing that mystics spend their time on.

KATHA UPANISHAD
THIRD VALLI[2]

1. 'There are the two, drinking their reward in the world of their own works, entered into the cave (of the heart), dwelling on the highest summit (the ether in the heart). Those who know Brahman call them shade and light; likewise, those householders who perform the Trinâkiketa sacrifice.'

2. 'May we be able to master that Nâkiketa rite which is a bridge for sacrificers; also that which is the highest, imperishable Brahman for those who wish to cross over to the fearless shore.'

---

2 Müller, Max. *The Sacred Books of the East*, vol. 15. Oxford: Oxford University Press, 1884.

3. 'Know the Self to be sitting in the chariot, the body to be the chariot, the intellect (buddhi) the charioteer, and the mind the reins.'

4. 'The senses they call the horses, the objects of the senses their roads. When he (the Highest Self) is in union with the body, the senses, and the mind, then wise people call him the Enjoyer.'

5. 'He who has no understanding and whose mind (the reins) is never firmly held, his senses (horses) are unmanageable, like vicious horses of a charioteer.'

6. 'But he who has understanding and whose mind is always firmly held, his senses are under control, like good horses of a charioteer.'

7. 'He who has no understanding, who is unmindful and always impure, never reaches that place, but enters into the round of births.'

8. 'But he who has understanding, who is mindful and always pure, reaches indeed that place, from whence he is not born again.'

9. 'But he who has understanding for his charioteer, and who holds the reins of the mind, he reaches the end of his journey, and that is the highest place of Vishnu.'

Analysis — Katha Upanishad, Third Valli

In line 1 we have several things going on. Firstly, it is to be noted that "ether," for the Hindus, means Brahman. So "the ether in the heart" is the mystical. Secondly, what is to be made of the phrase "cave of the heart?" Logically, it is nonsense. Surely there is no literally existing cave inside a person's heart. So we must interpret the phrase experientially.

Thirdly, what of the "shade" and "light" of which the mystics ("those who know Brahman") allegedly know? Here we have two archetypes, in a duality. The themes of light and darkness resonate throughout archetypal thinking. What do the terms signify?

"Nakiketa" refers to a ritual involving fire which the Hindus performed, and a "Trinakiketa" is apparently a person who has performed this ritual three times. These will be of little interest for us. It is common for people to ascribe mystical significance to particular acts and rituals, but in the absence of evidence we reject these ascriptions.

For the rest of line 2, we need only note the need to interpret "the fearless shore" experientially.

Line 3 introduces the concept of "Self." The Self, for the Hindus, is the Atman, or soul. It is a basic axiom of Hindu philosophy that Atman and Brahman are one. Therefore, metaphysics aside, the term Self means the mystical. Mystical texts feature many terms for one thing.

Here begins a complex metaphor. We have four philosophical concepts: the Self, the intellect (or buddhi), the mind, and the body. We imagine them in a stacked hierarchy: body on the bottom, then mind, then intellect, then Self at the top. These concepts can be interpreted in two ways: metaphysically, or archetypally.

In the metaphysical interpretation, we postulate that these four things literally exist: that besides our body, we literally have a thing called a mind, and then another distinct thing called an intellect, and then another distinct thing called a Self.

In the archetypal interpretation, we face the task of interpreting these terms as elements in our experience. The body and the Self are easy enough to interpret; the body is our body, and the Self is the mystical. What, then, are the mind and the intellect? These terms are hard to interpret because it is not clear (at least to me) what distinction is being made between "mind" and "intellect." If there were only one such concept on the playing field here, representing in general our thoughts and emotions and so forth, then matters would be clearer.

One possible interpretation is that "mind" refers to the feelings and emotions, while "intellect" refers to the thoughts.

Now let us examine the metaphor. We are given the image of a horse-drawn chariot. The Self is the master, the body the chariot, the intellect the driver, the mind the reins, the senses the horses, the objects of the senses the roads.

There are various directions in which we can take this metaphor. For instance, in this connection it seems that the Self is associated with the true will, that which knows where one really needs to be going. One then gets the idea that the chariot can be ill-managed: the horses misbehaving, the driver's hand off the reins, the driver not listening to the master, and so on.

If suitable archetypal associations can be found for these ideas, then they can constitute a basis for practical mystical thinking. One gets the advice that one needs one's horses under control, one needs the driver listening to the master, etc. In line 5 we get the advice that we need to control our emotions (hold the reins firmly), and control our senses (manage our horses). Furthermore, we are told that the achievement of this feat involves understanding, which we can tentatively postulate to be a state of the intellect.

Now let us examine the concept of the *Enjoyer* introduced in line 4. What does it mean for the Self to be in union with the body, the senses, and the mind? This can be made clearer if we interpret the Self as consciousness. (There is sense in the statement, "the mystical is consciousness.")

So, when consciousness is associated with the body, the senses, and the mind, this is the state in which the Self is called the *Enjoyer*. The only thing that is excluded from the Enjoyer is the intellect. So, we can simplify the idea by saying that the Self is the Enjoyer when it is in a sort of a thoughtless muddle of feeling and sensation, a state of lazy dreaminess.

The concept *Enjoyer* should be interpreted as another archetype. What does this word mean to an Upanishadic sage? We note the hostility to sensory pleasures which is a theme in Hindu mysticism, and the idea that one advances in one's spirituality by refraining from these. So the term *Enjoyer* is intended to evoke the antithesis of spiritual purity, a sort of state of depravity.

This idea is further advanced in line 5; we can tentatively postulate that "he who has no understanding" is also the Enjoyer.

In line 6 we get a description of the state of spiritual purity to contrast the depravity of the Enjoyer. It is characterized by understanding, control of the mind, and control of the senses.

So we can see that in this elaborate metaphor we are being given advice about the kind of mental state that a mystic benefits from. Whether or not this advice is good or useful is a matter to be left to an individual's discretion.

Lines 7 to 9 repeat the same contrast between the pure person and the impure person, introducing the idea that the impure person is trapped in the cycle of reincarnation, whereas the pure person escapes the cycle of reincarnation and reaches "that place." "That place" is presumably *moksha*, the final state of enlightenment posited by the Hindus, and the ultimate goodness which I postulated in the chapter *Rationality and Intuitions*.

Tao te Ching
Chapter 2[3]

1. When people see things as beautiful,
2. ugliness is created.
3. When people see things as good,
4. evil is created.

5. Being and non-being produce each other.
6. Difficult and easy complement each other.
7. Long and short define each other.
8. High and low oppose each other.
9. Fore and aft follow each other.

10. Therefore the Master
11. can act without doing anything
12. and teach without saying a word.
13. Things come her[4] way and she does not stop them;
14. things leave and she lets them go.
15. She has without possessing,
16. and acts without any expectations.
17. When her work is done, she takes no credit.
18. That is why it will last forever.

Analysis — Tao Te Ching, Chapter 2

The first nine lines of this chapter concern various dualities: beautiful/ugly, good/evil, being/non-being, difficult/easy, long/short, high/low, and fore/aft. The first four of these are clearly archetypes, while the last three have more of a mathematical character. (High/low also has an archetypal interpretation.)

Lao Tzu's basic objective in these nine lines seems to be to point out the inter-connectedness and mutual dependence of the opposites in every duality. A thing in a duality cannot exist without its opposite.

Consider line 7. Suppose I have a stick of length L. Is it long or short? The question has no answer. Now suppose I introduce another

---

[3] Translated for the public domain by J.H. McDonald, 1996. http://www.wright-house.com/religions/taoism/tao-te-ching.html

[4] The use of gender here is not meant to be interpreted literally. Masters can be both male and female.

stick, of length 2L. Now the first stick is "short," and the second stick is "long." If I introduce a third stick, of length $L/2$, then that stick will now be "short," and the first stick is no longer "short." One cannot have the concepts of "long" and "short" without multiple things of different lengths, and the *longness* or *shortness* of a thing is relative to what it is being compared to.

Now consider line 9. Suppose I have a moveable point, located somewhere in a plane. Which direction is forward, and which direction is back? The question has no answer. Now suppose that I move the point in some direction, in a straight line. Now "forward" and "back" exist. Forward is the direction I am going; back is the direction I am coming from. As soon as I create forward, I create backward, and vice versa. It is a logical impossibility for one to exist without the other.

Now we can create analogies in our intuition between these mathematical illustrations, and the more abstract cases of the archetypal dualities. If one cannot have long without short, or forward without backward, does it not make sense that one cannot have beautiful without ugly, or difficult without easy?

At line 10, Lao Tzu changes subjects, discussing the behavior of the Master. *The Master* is the one who is in perfect harmony with the Tao, which in our language is the mystical.

I ask myself why these two passages, apparently unconnected, are presented together in the same chapter. Why discuss the interdependence of opposites, and then abruptly shift to an apparently unrelated discussion of the behavior of the Master?

Reading between the lines, I infer that the Master chooses not to create these dualities. She does not create beauty, and so does not create ugliness. She does not create good, and so does not create evil. The Master lives in the world of non-duality, in the mystical.

Paradoxical capabilities are ascribed to the Master' she is able to "act without doing anything" (11), and "teach without saying a word" (12). These have both become tropes in Eastern philosophy.

The idea of acting without doing anything, or *wu-wei*, looms large in Eastern philosophy, and summarizes a significant portion of the entirety of Lao Tzu's practical advice. It is too large a subject to treat adequately here.

The idea of teaching without saying words is embodied in the Zen Buddhism tradition, where Zen masters use sideways, non-intellectual approaches to enlightening their students. (One thinks, for instance, of the stories of a Zen master hitting their student with a stick, and the student having a mystical experience.)

One may also understand line 12 as meaning that the Master's very way of being in the world is a statement of their wisdom, more powerful and eloquent than any words could be.

So much meaning can be interpreted into lines 11 and 12, given the surrounding cultural context, that any comment I could make on them would be a gross oversimplification.

Lines 13 to 16 describe the accepting, serene attitude of the Master.

Line 17 describes how the Master does not take pride in her work. Line 18 is a bit of a puzzle. Why would not taking pride in one's work result in it lasting forever?

It seems clear that line 18 is not to be taken literally. If I build a park, and do not take credit for building the park, that does not decrease the likelihood that the park will eventually be torn down or overrun by plants. Our attempt at a logical interpretation yields nonsense. This would seemingly indicate an experiential interpretation. But what is that interpretation?

One possibility is as follows. Pride is antithetical to mystical results. This is a perfectly verifiable claim, which anybody can discover for themselves by experiment. Taking pride in one's mystical results, therefore, hurts the possibility of having mystical results. Thus, it is because the Master does not take pride in her mystical work, that her mystical work meets with success. We say that the results of her work "last forever" simply because of the poetically eternal quality of the mystical.

This is one interpretation, but I am not wholly satisfied with it. Line 18 still remains a bit of a mystery to me.

Tao te ching
Chapter 77[5]

1. The Tao of heaven works in the world
2. like the drawing of a bow.
3. The top is bent downward;
4. the bottom is bent up.
5. The excess is taken from,

---

5 Translated for the public domain by J.H. McDonald, 1996. http://www.wright-house.com/religions/taoism/tao-te-ching.html

6. and the deficient is given to.
7. The Tao works to use the excess,
8. and gives to that which is depleted.
9. The way of the people is to take from the depleted,
10. and give to those who already have an excess.

11. Who is able to give to the needy from their excess?
12. Only someone who is following the way of the Tao.

13. This is why the Master gives
14. expecting nothing in return.
15. She does not dwell on her past accomplishments,
16. and does not glory in any praise.

Analysis — Tao Te Ching, Chapter 77

The image of "the drawing of a bow" given in line 2 leads us to imagine a straight line being bent inwards, approaching a circular shape. The bow can be taken as representing any duality. The drawing of the bow, then, represents the movement of that duality towards non-duality: the reduction of opposition, moving towards the unification of opposites.

In lines 5 and 6, we get a slightly more specific image, having to do with balancing. We imagine a pair of opposites in which one side is excessive, and the other is deficient, and we imagine correcting this imbalance.

This, "way of the Tao," is contrasted in lines 9 and 10 with "the way of the people," which is to exaggerate imbalances rather than correcting them. "The people" seem to be those who are uneducated or foolish, with the implication that this is the majority of people.

One idea which comes to mind with lines 9 and 10 is the way in which the rich get richer, and the poor get poorer; the powerful become more powerful, and the powerless have more power taken away. This can be taken as an especially obvious example of the general principle being discussed.

We can take the principle of balance being elucidated here as applicable both to external, material circumstances and to internal, psychological circumstances. It is possible through introspection to notice various dualities which characterize human psychology, and to notice that oneself stands imbalanced with respect to various of these dualities. Correcting these imbalances can be a part of mystical practice.

For instance, I know I am a very logical person, and the cost of this is that I have poorly developed intuitive faculties. Thus, I am imbalanced with respect to the duality logic/intuition, and I can work towards correcting this imbalance.

The implication of lines 11 and 12 seems to be that only a person who is following the mystical is capable of ethical action which corrects the imbalances in themselves and the world. This certainly seems not to be true a priori; but can we observe it to be true or false through analysis of our experience?

Lines 13 to 16 give us wisdom about how to act, which we can straightforwardly see to be good advice. As with the similar passage in Chapter 2 of the *Tao Te Ching*, the main challenge here is to figure out why this advice is juxtaposed with the principles expounded above it. Perhaps the reason that the Master gives while expecting nothing in return is that she knows that she is simply doing what is necessary, correcting any imbalance and not having any attachment to the outcome.

THE DHAMMAPADA
CHAPTER 1
THE TWIN VERSES[6]

1. All that we are is the result of what we have thought: it is founded on our thoughts, it is made up of our thoughts. If a man speaks or acts with an evil thought, pain follows him, as the wheel follows the foot of the ox that draws the carriage.

2. All that we are is the result of what we have thought: it is founded on our thoughts, it is made up of our thoughts. If a man speaks or acts with a pure thought, happiness follows him, like a shadow that never leaves him.

3. 'He abused me, he beat me, he defeated me, he robbed me,'—in those who harbour such thoughts hatred will never cease.

4. 'He abused me, he beat me, he defeated me, he robbed me,'—in those who do not harbour such thoughts hatred will cease.

5. For hatred does not cease by hatred at any time: hatred ceases by love, this is an old rule.

---

6 Müller, Max. *The Sacred Books of the East*, vol. 10. Oxford: Oxford University Press, 1881.

Analysis — The Dhammapada, Chapter 1

Taken in cultural context, this passage is connected with the concept of *karma*. According to this concept, a person travels through a series of incarnations, and throughout these incarnations they are followed by their thoughts and actions.

Good thoughts and actions yield "good karma," which results in leading a happy life. Bad thoughts and actions yield "bad karma," which results in leading an unhappy life.

The concept of karma is a complex one, which probably means different things to different people. It mixes psychological facts that we can observe in our experience together with unverifiable metaphysical claims.

Some believers in karma hold that a person who is experiencing unfortunate material circumstances is receiving punishment for bad karma, and that a person who is experiencing fortunate material circumstances is receiving a reward for good karma. This is one metaphysical aspect of the concept of karma.

In attempting to enact the *principle of charitability*, we ought to find some aspect of the concept being elucidated here which we can observe to be true based on our own experience.

In grasping the meaning of this text, it is important that we understand what is meant by "thought," by "pure thought," and by "evil thought." This, of course, is not made perfectly clear; so we must extrapolate.

Each of these terms delineates some set of psychological phenomena; therefore they are to be interpreted archetypally. Lines 3 and 4 give hints as to how to interpret them.

A "thought" seems to be a way of interpreting our experience. We can interpret our experience in a positive, loving manner (a "pure thought"), or we can interpret our experience in a negative, hateful manner (an "evil thought").

The words "belief" or "bias" seem to be fairly close to the mark — also the Buddhist concept of *samskāra*. But we are merely throwing more words at the problem; the referent for the term must be rooted out in our own experience.

Part of the message of the text seems to be that interpreting experience in a positive manner leads to happiness, while interpreting experience in a negative manner leads to pain. We can observe on reflection that this is perfectly true. One who holds hatred and resentments keeps negativity alive in themselves. One who loves and forgives keeps positivity alive in themselves. Our own suffering or absence of suffering is a function of how we choose to feel about our lives and the world.

The heart sutra[7]

When Avalokiteśvara Bodhisattva was practicing the profound Prajñāpāramitā, he illuminated the Five Skandhas and saw that they were all empty, and crossed over all suffering and affliction.

"Śāriputra, form is not different from emptiness, and emptiness is not different from form. Form itself is emptiness, and emptiness itself is form. Sensation, conception, synthesis, and discrimination are also such as this. Śāriputra, all phenomena are empty: they are neither created nor destroyed, neither defiled nor pure, and they neither increase nor diminish. This is because in emptiness there is no form, sensation, conception, synthesis, or discrimination. There are no eyes, ears, nose, tongue, body, or thoughts. There are no forms, sounds, scents, tastes, sensations, or phenomena. There is no field of vision and there is no realm of thoughts. There is no ignorance nor elimination of ignorance, even up to and including no old age and death, nor elimination of old age and death. There is no suffering, its accumulation, its elimination, or a path. There is no understanding and no attaining.

"Because there is no attainment, bodhisattvas rely on Prajñāpāramitā, and their minds have no obstructions. Since there are no obstructions, they have no fears. Because they are detached from backwards dream-thinking, their final result is Nirvāṇa. Because all buddhas of the past, present, and future rely on Prajñāpāramitā, they attain Anuttarā Samyaksaṃbodhi. Therefore, know that Prajñāpāramitā is a great spiritual mantra, a great brilliant mantra, an unsurpassed mantra, and an unequalled mantra. The Prajñāpāramitā Mantra is spoken because it can truly remove all afflictions. The mantra is spoken thusly:

gate, gate, pāragate, pārasaṃgate, bodhi svāhā

---

[7] Translated for the public domain by Lapis Lazuli Texts. http://www.lapislazulitexts.com/T08_0251.html

Analysis — The Heart Sutra

Firstly, what is a "bodhisattva?" This word appears to have two principal interpretations in Buddhism. The first is as an individual who is enlightened — who has achieved some final and permanent state of mystical attainment. The second is as an individual who has a desire to attain enlightenment and works towards this goal, motivated by compassion for the suffering of all beings.

With the first interpretation we run up against the following question: is there such a state, and is it attainable by humans in this lifetime?

With the second interpretation, the concept "Bodhisattva" becomes more or less a Buddhist spin on the concept "mystic."

Avalokiteśvara is the — apparently mythical — bodhisattva who made a great vow to assist all sentient beings in times of difficulty, and to postpone his own Buddhahood until he has assisted every being on Earth in achieving Nirvāṇa.

Now, how are we to interpret the word "Prajñāpāramitā?" It translates literally as "perfection of transcendent wisdom." Prajñāpāramitā is understood, in Mahayana Buddhism, as the highest truth which Buddhism has to offer. It is what is elucidated in texts called Prajñāpāramitā sutras, of which the current text is one.

Though I am not deeply familiar with this topic, it seems to me that the basic concept of Prajñāpāramitā is non-dualism.

One begins by stating that all phenomena are "empty." What do the writers mean by "empty?"[8] "Emptiness" is probably the mystical. So to say that all phenomena are empty, is to say that all phenomena are the mystical. This is non-dualism.

One then goes on to obliterate any distinction between emptiness and non-emptiness; between enlightenment and non-enlightenment; and so forth. All concepts and distinctions are systematically abolished. This is, again, non-dualism.

The reader may recall that I consider non-dualism to be a valid concept, as long as it is interpreted experientially and not metaphysically. To interpret it experientially is to experience the world through this point of view. To interpret it metaphysically is

---

[8] The Dalai Lama states that at the heart of emptiness is the deep recognition that there is a fundamental disparity between the way we perceive the world, including our own experience in it, and the way things actually are. — Ed.

to say that all phenomena really are empty: that a chair is really the mystical, that a glass of water is really the mystical, etc. (Do we therefore infer that a chair is really a glass of water? If so, then why do I not sit on a glass of water?)

In defining the term "Prajñāpāramitā," we explain at one stroke the essential meaning of the Heart Sutra. But let us examine further.

What are the "Five Skandhas?" They are five categories of phenomena. In Buddhism, it is believed that all phenomena fall into one of these five categories. The Sanskrit names for the Five Skandhas are rūpa, vedanā, samjñā, samskāra, and vijñāna. In this text, they are translated as form, sensation, conception, synthesis, and discrimination.

Here we have a choice between applying a metaphysical interpretation, or applying an archetypal interpretation. By the *principle of charitability*, we apply the archetypal interpretation. So, we must identify what aspects of our subjective experience these terms refer to.

I have personally spent a great deal of time studying the Five Skandhas from an archetypal perspective. Here I summarize the interpretations which I eventually arrived at.

Every subjective experience partakes of all five Skandhas. Let us consider, for the sake of argument, the experience of looking at a tree:

The "form" is the outline, contours, texture, colors, etc., of the tree.

The "sensation" is the perception of good feelings or bad feelings associated with the phenomenon. In this case, perhaps I feel a good feeling of beauty in connection with the tree.

The "conception" is the intellectual understanding connected with the phenomenon. In this case it would be the wordless, intellectual understanding that "this is a tree," subtly connecting it to everything that I know about trees.

The "synthesis" is the set of basic, subconscious mental factors and biases which predispose me to perceive a tree.

The "discrimination" is the fact of my consciousness itself -- the fact that there is a perception at all, as opposed to the silence of death or deep sleep.

Having interpreted the key concepts of Prajñāpāramitā, emptiness, and the Five Skandhas, there is little work left to be done on the Heart Sutra.

Let us complete our interpretation of the first paragraph. Why does it say that the Bodhisattva "crossed over all suffering and affliction?" In Buddhism it is generally held that the purpose of mystical attainment is to end the suffering of oneself and others. This line is present because of the Buddhist idea that mystical attainment ends suffering.

Here we have a perfectly testable claim. Does attaining the mystical and realizing the poetic truth of non-dualism allow one to end one's suffering? Why not find out?

The second paragraph is an elaboration of material we have already covered.

In the final paragraph, the term "Nirvāna"[9] refers again to a hypothetical final, permanent state of mystical attainment. "Anuttarā Samyaksambodhi" refers to the same.

Near the end the text begins to equate the concept "Prajñāpāramitā" with a certain mantra, reading "gate, gate, paragate, parasamgate, bodhi svaha." This translates as "gone, gone, gone beyond, beyond going beyond, hail the enlightened one." We can see that this is a rendition, in mantra form, of the idea of Prajñāpāramitā, and a condensation of the basic message of the Heart Sutra.

OAHSPE
BOOK OF JEHOVIH
CHAPTER I[10]

1. ALL was. ALL is. ALL ever shall be. The ALL spake, and Motion was, and is, and ever shall be; and, being positive, was called He and Him. The ALL MOTION was His speech.

2. He said, I AM! And He comprehended all things, the seen and the unseen. Nor is there aught in all the universe but what is part of Him.

3. He said, I am the soul of all; and the all that is seen is of My person and My body.

4. By virtue of My presence all things are. By virtue of My presence is life. By virtue of My presence are the living brought forth into life. I am the QUICKENER, the MOVER, the CREATOR, the DESTROYER. I am FIRST and LAST.

---

9 Buddhists believe that nirvana is not a goal or destination but more like a series of undoings - Ed.
10 Newbrough, John Ballou. Oahspe: A New Bible. Newbrough, 1882.

5. Of two apparent entities am I, nevertheless I AM BUT ONE. These entities are the UNSEEN, which is POTENT, and the SEEN, which is of itself IMPOTENT, and called CORPER.

6. With these two entities, in likeness thereby of Myself, made I all the living; for as the life is the potent part, so is the corporeal part the impotent part.

7. Chief over all that live on the earth I made Man; male and female made I them. And that man might distinguish Me, I commanded him to give Me a name; by virtue of my presence commanded I him. And man named Me not after anything in heaven or on the earth. In obedience to My will named he Me after the sounds the wind uttereth, and he said E-O-Ih! Which is now pronounced Jehovih, and is written thus (Fig 9):

Fig. 9: The Symbol of Jehovih

ANALYSIS — OAHSPE, BOOK OF JEHOVIH

This highly metaphysical passage describes the creation of the universe from the "ALL." The ALL can be understood as the mystical. We thus see a repetition of the trope that everything comes from the mystical.

Line 1 describes the ALL as timeless, which has a valid experiential interpretation.

Line 1 describes how Motion emerges from the ALL. We can understand Motion as an archetype. Motion is described as positive and male, these being archetypal attributions.

Line 2 says, "He said, I AM!" The I AM, being the ALL's speech, would seem to be Motion. We can further extrapolate that "I" is the ALL, and "AM" is Motion.

Line 2 repeats the metaphysical idea that all things come from the ALL. (Phrased this way, it appears to be a tautology.)

Line 2 first establishes the duality seen/unseen. Again we may interpret this metaphysically or archetypally. A likely metaphysical interpretation is that "the seen" is the world that we experience, and "the unseen" is an additional, hidden, noumenal aspect to the world.

We may take this as the point of departure for an archetypal interpretation. I suggest the following archetypal associations to enrich these concepts, based on my own intuition. The seen is ethereality, light, maleness, consciousness. The unseen is solidity, darkness, femaleness, unconsciousness.

Line 3, and the first two sentences of line 4, repeat basic features of the ideas being discussed.

The third and fourth sentences of line 4 give epithets for the ALL suggesting metaphysical or archetypal attributes.

Line 5 reiterates the seen/unseen duality, also naming it potent/impotent, thus further enriching the concept.

Line 6 suggests that all living things exist as a unity of the seen and the unseen. This is difficult to interpret archetypally. Taking the living thing as a plant, we may imagine the unseen as the solid ground in which it grows, and the seen as the air and light upon which it feeds. But how are we to relate this to our experience?

We may take a "living thing" as any psychological phenomenon. We may then understand line 6 as describing psychological phenomena as a unity of the revealing abstraction of consciousness with the revealed complexity of unconscious material.

Line 7 gives three names for the ALL: E-O-Ih!, Jehovih, and a picture which is a mandala containing a leaf. The first name seems designed to be chanted, and one is reminded of the meme that certain sounds have mystical significance.

Helena blavatsky
Isis Unveiled
Part Two, Chapter I
Page 39

"The holy primitive syllable, composed of the three letters **A — U — M**, in which is contained the Vedic Trimurti (Trinity), must be kept secret, like another triple Veda," says Manu, in book xi., sloka 265.

Swayambhouva is the unrevealed Deity; it is the Being existent through and of itself; he is the central and immortal germ of all that exists in the universe. Three trinities emanate and are confounded in him, forming a Supreme unity. These trinities, or the triple Trimurti, are: the Nara, Nari, and Viradyi--the initial triad; the Agni, Vaya, and Sourya--the manifested triad; Brahma, Vishnu, and Siva, the creative triad. Each of these triads becomes less metaphysical and more adapted to the vulgar intelligence as it descends. Thus the last becomes but the symbol in its concrete expression; the necessarianism of a purely meta-physical conception. Together with Swayambhouva, they are the ten Sephiroth of the Hebrew kabalists, the ten Hindu Prajapatis--the En-Soph of the former, answering to the great Unknown, expressed by the mystic **A U M**, (Fig. 10), of the latter.

Fig. 10: The AUM

ANALYSIS — HELENA BLAVATSKY, ISIS UNVEILED

The quote from Manu accomplishes three things. First, Manu ascribes mystical significance to the syllable AUM. We may take AUM as representing the mystical, as this is how it is used throughout Hindu literature. In the absence of evidence, we reject the claim that there is anything special about this particular syllable, beyond the fact that people consider it to be special.

Second, Manu considers AUM split into its three component letters, regarding these as representing the Trimurti. The Trimurti is a trinity of Hindu gods: Brahma the creator, Vishnu the preserver, and Shiva the destroyer.

Third, Manu asserts that the syllable AUM must be kept secret. The idea of secret, hidden knowledge is a common meme in mysticism.

The phrase "another triple Veda" probably refers to three Hindu sacred texts: the Rigveda, the Yajurveda, and the Samaveda. So Manu is also claiming that these books must be kept secret.

Unfortunately for Manu, the cat is quite out of the bag on all of these things!

Swayambhouva seems to be the mystical. Blavatsky paints a picture for us of a descending spiral of three trinities emanating from Swayambhouva. I don't have the slightest idea what she means when she says, "the last becomes but the symbol in its concrete expression; the necessarianism of a purely meta-physical conception."

She equates the whole construction with the ten Sephiroth of the Tree of Life, and with the ten Hindu Prajapatis. The Hindu Prajapatis are gods of procreation. She also equates the three veils of negative existence of the Tree of Life with the three letters of the syllable AUM.

These equations are fairly characteristic of mystical thinking: drawing parallels between concepts from different traditions, with the object of showing that they are describing the same thing. The idea is that when such parallels can be found, it validates all of the concepts under discussion.

As usual, we can interpret Blavatsky's ideas metaphysically, or archetypally. If we wish to interpret them archetypally, we must find things in our experience with which to correlate to each of her concepts. I am not confident that this can be done, with the level to which she has specified the concepts in question.

I am also skeptical of her equations with the Tree of Life and the Prajapatis. The most damning fact is that she does not specify precisely to which Sephira, or to which Prajapati, each of her concepts corresponds! More generally, I doubt that her proposed equations can be brought to the point of resonating in archetypal harmony. Is there really a Prajapati sufficiently similar to each Sephira to assemble an experientially satisfying system that correlates the two concept complexes? I suspect not. My hypothesis is that Blavatsky equated these systems simply because all of them contained ten concepts.

My judgment, therefore, is that the whole passage is probably humbug.

Emerald Tablet of Hermes Trismegistus[11]

1. Truly, without error, certainly and most truly:
2. That which is below is as that which is above, and that which is above is as that which is below, towards the performance of the miracle of the one thing.
3. And as all things come from one, through the meditation of the one, so all things are born out of this one thing, through transformation.
4. Its father is the Sun. Its mother is the Moon.
5. The wind carried It in its belly. Its food is the earth.
6. The father of all consecrated things is this.
7. Its power is whole if it is turned into earth.
8. Separate earth from fire, subtle from coarse, lovingly, with great intelligence.
9. It ascends from earth into heaven, once more descends into earth, and receives the power of things above and things below.
10. Thus it governs the glory of the whole world.
11. Thereby it leaves behind all obscurity.
12. This is the true power of all powers, because it conquers all subtle things, and penetrates all solid things.
13. Thus is the world created.
14. From this will be miraculous transformations, of which this is the method. Therefore I am named Hermes Trisgmegistus, having the three-part philosophy of the whole world.
15. My speech about the working of the Sun is finished.

Analysis — Emerald Tablet

The usual interpretation of line 2 is as expressing the analogy between the microcosm ("that which is below") and the macrocosm ("that which is above"). According to this principle, the microcosm and the macrocosm are isomorphic in structure.

"Microcosm" and "macrocosm" can mean various things. A common interpretation is that the microcosm is a person, and the macrocosm is God. In this case, the principle is expressed in the Biblical idea that God created man in His own image.

More generally, we can understand the macrocosm as the whole, and the microcosm as the part. Thus, for instance, if we take the

---

11 My own translation for the public domain, from the Latin by Chrysogonus Polydorus, 1541.

universe as the macrocosm, we can take galaxies as microcosms. If we take galaxies as macrocosmos, we can take stars and planets as microcosmos. If we take planets as macrocosmos, we can take living organisms as microcosmos. If we take living organisms as macrocosmos, we can take individual cells as microcosmos. If we take cells as macrocosmos, then we can take atoms as microcosmos.

Thus, the principle "that which is below is as that which is above" can be understood as stating, essentially, that existence has a fractal structure, in which the parts follow the same design as the whole. A star is in some fundamental way like a galaxy, an organism in some fundamental way like a planet, a cell in some fundamental way like an organism, etc.

We can see specific cases in which our knowledge shows this to be true. Taking a human society as the macrocosm, and people as microcosmos, we can say that a single person contains in miniature the information embodied in their culture as a whole. Taking a living organism as the macrocosm, and cells as microcosmos, we can say that a single cell contains — in the form of DNA — the information needed to construct the entire organism.

Unfortunately, the idea of the analogy between microcosm and macrocosm, if extended beyond such specific cases and into its full generality, is metaphysics. Future advances in knowledge may clarify and vindicate the principle. But, at our present state of knowledge, and despite the elegance of the idea, it is firmly in the area of vague speculation.

There is another sense in which we can interpret line 2, which is archetypal instead of metaphysical, and which conveys a very different — though familiar — idea.

This text is replete with dualities which are variations on the duality high/low. We see heaven/earth (line 9), fire/earth (line 8), wind/earth (line 5), subtle/coarse (line 8), and subtle/solid (line 12). High is similar to heaven is similar to fire is similar to wind is similar to subtle. Low is similar to earth is similar to coarse is similar to solid. So these dualities are all variations on each other.

There is an archetypal association between highness and the mystical, and between lowness and the negation of the mystical. One thinks, for instance, of the fact that God is in heaven, and Satan is in hell. Furthermore, there is an archetypal association between "high" and "better," and between "low" and "worse." (A "high score," a "high rank," a "low blow," "stooping to his level," etc.) Since the mystical is the best thing, it is also the highest thing.

Matters are somewhat confused by the fact that the mystical is non-dual. Thus, it is true that the mystical is the highest, and simultaneously true that the mystical is both high and low. This would be very confusing, if not for the fact that we in the domain of experience (as in all discussions of archetypes), and therefore we do not demand logical consistency.

The duality "that which is above"/"that which is below" can be taken as a high/low duality. Under this archetypal interpretation, what does it mean to say "that which is above is as that which is below?" It can be understood as an equation of the opposites high and low: an expression of the concept of non-duality.

This interpretation is reinforced when we examine the rest of line 2, which reads, "towards the performance of the miracle of the one thing." We can interpret "the one thing" as the mystical. "The miracle of the one thing," then, can be interpreted as mystical experience. Under this interpretation, line 2 states, roughly, that the uniting of opposites leads to mystical experience.

Line 3 states that all things come from the one thing. We can interpret this as the familiar metaphysical idea that everything comes from the mystical.

Lines 4 and 5 describe the origins of the one thing. There is an obvious metaphysical interpretation, which is that the one thing was literally the child of the sun and moon, and literally was cradled by the wind and fed on earth. We will ignore this interpretation by the *principle of charitability*.

There is an apparent inconsistency between these lines, and line 3. Line 3 states that the one thing is the source of all things; and then lines 4 and 5 go on to state the sources of the one thing. How can the one thing come from anything if everything comes from it? A looser, experiential interpretation is apparently required to resolve the inconsistency. We can understand all as coming from the one thing, and we can also understand the one thing as the sum of all. There is only a contradiction if we think in terms of a chain of causality leading from the one thing to all things, or from the sun, the moon, etc., to the one thing. Any such concept of a chain of causality would, of course, be metaphysics.

In light of these comments, let us find a non-metaphysical interpretation for line 4. I suggest that we take Sun/Moon as an archetypal duality. This particular duality is similar to the dualities male/female and light/dark. The idea that this duality births the one thing can then be understood as being true in the sense that the mystical is a union of opposites.

Now, what of line 5? The duality wind/earth is one of the high/low dualities. We can then interpret line 5 similarly to line 4, describing the one thing as a union of opposites.

Line 6 describes the one thing as the source of everything (experientially) holy.

Line 7 is a bit mystifying, but can perhaps be interpreted as meaning that the one thing's potential is fulfilled when it is manifested in the world, when the profane is made holy.

Line 8 contains more high/low dualities: namely, fire/earth, and subtle/coarse. We are instructed to "separate earth from fire, [and] subtle from coarse." We may interpret this as an instruction to distinguish intellectually between that which is holy, and that which is profane.

Line 9 seems to be describing the mystical as vibrating between heaven and earth. We can certainly poetically understand the mystical as such a vibration. There is also a clear allusion to the idea of non-duality, of the mystical uniting these opposites.

Line 10 seems to reiterate the general idea of line 6.

Line 11 is straightforward to interpret.

Line 12 states, "this [the one thing] is the true power of all powers." This means, firstly, that the one thing is true power, as opposed to various chimeras which appear to be power but really are not. It means, secondly, that all powers derive their power from the one thing. It is not clear in what, if any, sense this is verifiably the case.

Line 13 seems to repeat the metaphysical idea from line 3.

Line 14 states, "from this will be miraculous transformations, of which this is the method." The same word, "transformation," is used in line 3 to refer to the means by which all things are derived from the one thing.

Thus, we can interpret "this" as meaning the one thing, and line 14 as reiterating the idea that all things come from it.

We can also interpret "miraculous transformations" as referring to mystical results, in which case line 14 states that the method laid out in the text will lead to mystical results.

Finally, we can interpret "miraculous transformations" as referring to magical results: i.e., the manifestation of paranormal phenomena. The alchemists, who often regarded this text as a treatise on alchemy, took such an interpretation. They believed that turning lead into gold was one of the "transformations" possible through the method laid out here. We reject such claims, in the absence of good evidence.

This completes our discussion of mystical thinking. We have seen that mysticism is a topic which is difficult to think carefully about, and that this results in texts which are both ambiguous in their meaning and questionable in their correctness. By approaching mysticism in a rational fashion, we can lessen this problem. We can clarify our thoughts and be better equipped to notice problems.

We have also seen that mystical thinking follows patterns. Much of it we can think of as discussion of archetypes; and it is most largely concerned with one subject, which is the mystical. Noticing these patterns can again help to clarify what is being said.

Having finished with mystical thinking, we will now turn briefly to the practical aspect of mysticism — that is, the attempt to achieve mystical experiences.

"All of you who are worth your salt will be absolutely delighted when I tell you to scrap all the rules and discover your own."

- Aleister Crowley, Eight Lectures on Yoga

7

MYSTICAL PRACTICES

As stated in the *Introduction*, mystical practices are anything done to induce mystical experiences. Such practices include meditation, prayer, various types of ritual, dancing, music, ingestion of drugs, modification of breathing, fasting, sensory deprivation, techniques involving sexuality, and so forth. Such practices seem to have been done in virtually every culture, and there is not a great deal of difference in the practices between cultures.

This book requires that we consider mystical practices in relation to rationality and there are many traditional approaches to mystical practice. Does rationality recommend that we do anything differently from how things are normally done? As it happens, it does. In this chapter I will explain how.

My intent in this chapter is not to lay down everything that I know about mystical practice, as that subject would require a book of its own for a proper treatment. So I restrict myself largely to thinking about the relationship between mystical practice and rationality.

My suggested approach to mystical practice can be summarized in a sentence: *Take nothing on faith, and apply your own intelligence and creativity in determining how to practice.*

Instructions for various mystical practices abound in literature. They instruct one on how to sit, how to breathe, what movements to perform, what words to say, what images to visualize, and even how to decorate the room in which one practices. They also say what to eat, what one's sex life should be like, and even, I once found, whether to sleep on one's side or on one's back.

In experimenting with these different conditions, I came to conclude that none of them mattered very much. There is nothing simple, easy to describe, and easy to do which makes a significant difference in the effectiveness of one's practice.

There are no magic bullets. There is no special, secret exercise out there somewhere which, if performed, will suddenly make things much easier and better. There is nothing special about any mantra. There is nothing really important about how one sits, or what signs one makes with one's hands. Experimenting with these conditions, in my experience, does not lead anywhere.

There are some simple conditions that really do seem to be important for mystical practice. In my experience, it is helpful to have a specific place dedicated to practice. It is obviously necessary that this place be quiet and free of interruptions. It is necessary to be physically comfortable. It is better to practice while fully awake, and without a full stomach, as both of these conditions inhibit mental alertness. Regulating one's breathing really does seem to have various effects. I recommend not trusting me on any of these statements; rather, I suggest verifying them for yourself.

Much of the irrationality in the field of mystical practice seems to come from reliance on authority. One assumes that a particular source is trustworthy, and does what that source says, without examining any of the issues for oneself. We should not rely on authority; we should understand what we are doing, base our beliefs on evidence, and apply our intelligence to the task. We should form hypotheses, perform experiments, observe the results of the experiments, and revise our hypotheses accordingly.

All of these different recommendations we have examined for the conditions of mystical practice skirt around the edges of the issue, without addressing the essence. Generally, the literature surrounding the topic does precisely this. What are the essential — as opposed to the peripheral — conditions which induce mystical experiences?

It seems to me that this question of the essence cannot really be discussed. This, I infer, is the reason that the literature always focuses on peripheral issues. One can indeed learn the technique of inducing mystical experiences. But this technique, it seems to me, is not something that can be set down in language, or taught to another. It is far too intuitive, too instinctive, too complex, too variable based on the situation. Can one explain how to write a great poem? One cannot. Similarly, one cannot explain how to have a mystical experience. It is an art, not a science.

We are not surprised that there is no systematic procedure for making a great work of art. We would ridicule anybody who offered up such a procedure, and assume that the procedure did not work. But for some reason we find it easy to believe that there is a systematic procedure for inducing mystical experiences. We may even *expect* there to be such a procedure, and be surprised if somebody says that there is not. Why this inconsistency?

There is not a systematic procedure for doing anything remarkable. There is no systematic procedure for loving another person; no systematic procedure for making a great scientific discovery; no systematic procedure for gaining political power; no systematic procedure for coming to know oneself. Having mystical experiences is not less remarkable than these other things. Why, then, would anybody think that there was a systematic procedure for inducing mystical experiences?

This may seem like a cop-out, a way to avoid actually giving any guidance on the problem. But we can only make progress on the problem when we have recognized what the problem really is. The problem is not one of finding a magic bullet. The problem is much deeper, much subtler, and much more personal. If one actually approaches the problem, with one's own creativity and intelligence, under the assumption that there is no simple solution — then one can make progress on it. But one must realize the nature of the problem.

I might go so far, therefore, as to say that all instructions for mystical practices, written, verbal, or demonstrated, are mostly useless. I doubt that there is much that can be learned from any of them. What is essential in mystical practice cannot be taught; what can be taught is mostly periphery, accident, and arbitrary convention.

There are various psychological factors which dispose against taking this perspective on mystical practice. The perspective that there are no magic bullets or easily understandable methods makes the problem of mystical practice seem much harder. It becomes the kind of the problem that people usually look at, think about for a bit, and then give up on because it's too perplexing.

My position, of course, is that taking this perspective only makes the problem *seem* harder. Since, in my opinion, this perspective is the truth, the problem of mystical practice has been this hard all along. In taking this perspective, we only own up to the real difficulty of the problem. Furthermore, by recognizing the true nature of the problem, we increase our odds of making progress on it.

When I offer the advice that one ought to use one's own intelligence to determine how to practice, there is the risk that one will interpret me as meaning that one ought to sit around intellectualizing about how to practice. This would probably not do as much good as practicing and performing experiments would. One does not learn how to play the guitar by sitting around thinking about the most theoretically optimal way to play a guitar. Mystical practice is basically not an intellectual activity, though the intellect can be a tool which one applies in it.

When I say to apply your intelligence, the word "intelligence" encompasses quite a bit more than the intellectual intelligence with which one follows lines of reasoning and solves logic problems. It includes instincts, intuitions, emotional intelligence, and other things for which psychologists do not have names. Every mental faculty that one has is to be bent towards the problem.

It is because of my belief that there are no magic bullets or teachable methods that I have over time been attracted to meditation as my favored mystical practice. Prayer and ritual both seem to necessarily contain elements that are arbitrary. I am not prepared to say that nobody ought to use prayer or ritual. But, I have personally abandoned them.

If one does include arbitrary elements in one's practices, it seems to me that at best, these elements be as consistent as possible. If one uses a ritual, it is probably best if one repeats that same ritual for years. The ritual will tend to grow in power over time.

If one uses symbols in one's practices, it is best if these symbols have archetypal meanings. Consider, by way of illustration, the Lesser Banishing Ritual of the Pentagram. In this ritual, one chants words while performing various gestures and acts. The first words are, "ateh, malkuth, ve geburah, ve gedulah."

Each of these words is an archetype. "Ateh" means "thou art," and represents the mystical. "Malkuth" means "kingdom," and represents the world. "Geburah" means "power," and "gedulah" means "mercy." These archetypes form two dualities: ateh/malkuth, and geburah/gedulah. By vividly imagining each of these archetypes while intoning the corresponding word, one can make an effective ritual.

One of the problems with using a deliberate, structured method ("perform this ritual," "repeat this mantra," and so on) is that it closes off the opportunity for spontaneously using what is present in the moment. In mystical practice one is attempting to shape constantly varying mental circumstances towards a somewhat less varying goal. The shortest path from one's present point to one's goal is therefore a highly contingent matter. If one does not structure one's mystical practice according to a strict mental regimen, then one has the opportunity to use to one's advantage of the creative potential present in the spontaneity of an unrestricted mind.

Concentration and Relaxation

One thing that does seem to be essential to mystical practices is mental concentration. Meditation, prayer, and ritual all have this in common: they involve mental concentration. One can verify by experiment that concentrating one's mind does indeed tend to produce mystical results.

For a long time, I subscribed to the theory that concentration was all there was to mystical practice, and that achieving higher levels of concentration was the way to achieve better results.

According to this theory, all one had to do in mystical practice was to concentrate on something. What to concentrate on? I went with Aleister Crowley's theory, according to which it was best to concentrate on something in itself meaningless, so as to avoid falling into the trap of thinking that there was something specially significant about the object of concentration. Thus I used an imagined red triangle as my object of concentration.

I now believe that the concentration theory of mystical practice is false. It was not borne out by my experiments. I found cases in which intense concentration did not produce mystical results, and cases in which mystical results occurred in the absence of concentration.

It seems to me that concentration is an important element of mystical practice; but it is an element, and not the entirety of the process.

An error I made in my previous approach to concentration was that of thinking that the proper approach was to concentrate as intensely as possible, at full blast for the whole meditation. This is not even possible; attention is a limited resource, which one eventually runs out of. One cannot be a spendthrift with this mental resource, so it is much better if we can find a technique which does not take a heavy toll on it.

An additional — and perhaps more serious — problem with this approach is that the mental spaciousness and openness which comes from not concentrating, but instead relaxing, seems to be helpful as well. Some approaches to meditation recommend relaxing mentally and not making any efforts. I have found that there is something to be gained from this mental attitude.

This is a bit of a paradox. Some meditation techniques recommend concentration, and others recommend relaxation, though concentration and relaxation are opposites. Furthermore, experiment will confirm that both of these seem to work, though neither works perfectly or reliably. I was puzzled by this paradox for a long time.

The best approach, so far as I have found from my experiments, lies somewhere in between these extremes. It is not a matter of staking out a middle ground between concentration and relaxation. Rather, it is a matter of artfully using concentration and relaxation as part of the dance. One concentrates when the moment demands it, and relaxes when the moment demands it.

To perform a dance does not require tensing all of one's muscles, or relaxing all of one's muscles; it requires tensing and relaxing one's muscles in a graceful, natural, and artful pattern. Similarly, in meditation, one needs to tense or relax one's "mental muscles" in a graceful, natural, and artful pattern.

Of course, it would be useless to take as one's mystical technique, "concentrate and relax in an artful pattern." Similarly, the sentence "tense and relax your muscles in an artful pattern" is not an instruction for performing a dance. It is necessary, but not sufficient; if it is all that you have said, you have not yet said enough to specify the task.

The fact that concentration and relaxation are involved in mystical practice does not mean that one needs to think about them. Just as a dancer might never need to think, "now I shall tense my left calf muscle," a mystic might never need to think, "now I shall concentrate." This thought could prove useful; but it is not necessary.

Living in the Mystical

Mysticism is not a discipline, like disciplines such as mathematics, or painting, or tennis, which can be pursued as an isolated activity separate from the rest of one's life. A person cannot move forward in mysticism while everything else about them remains in one place. Rather, the successful mystic will inevitably become a different person.

In broaching this subject we first encounter the fact that mysticism is entirely integrated into the devoted mystic's life. There is no aspect of the mystic's life which mysticism does not touch in some way. Mysticism is, for the mystic, is not only a set of experiences, practices, and beliefs; it is a way of living, which reaches out its tendrils to influence everything.

A complete guide to mystical practice, then, would necessarily be a guide to life. Much has been written, in mystical literature, about how to live. Books such as the Bible and the *Tao Te Ching* speak to this question, providing us with ethical principles which we may follow, which provide us with guidance for diverse situations.

It seems to me that a significant portion of the problem lies in this area. Much of what one needs to know in order to meditate is universally applicable; the principles which tell one how to meditate also tell one how to talk to a friend, how to wash the dishes, and how to write a computer program. So the question is not only one of specific mental techniques, but one of general ethical principles.

What are these principles? I have a great deal to say on this deep and important topic; but to say it would require writing another book. I could choose, in this text, to give a partial and inadequate treatment of my thoughts on the matter. Instead, I prefer to remain silent. In a future book, I will say it better than I could say it here.

The main purpose of this book is to solve the conflict between rationality and mysticism. Thus, in my treatment of mysticism, I have given only an outline. I have stated that there are archetypes, without explaining the specific archetypes that I study. I have stated that there are ethical principles, without explaining the specific ethical principles to which I adhere. What has been laid out here is in the nature of a foundation; but I intend for future works to build upon it.

PART TWO

DUALITY AND NON-DUALITY

SO far we have held mysticism at arm's length, saying much about it without ever involving ourselves in it. Now we will change our angle, and delve into the depths of mystical thought.

The following chapters are attempts to express some of the ideas which have been stimulated in me by my practice of mysticism. They are attempts to express the inexpressible. The reader is encouraged to interpret the text along the lines which I have laid out in *Part One*.

Much of the text is concerned with the concepts of duality and non-duality, and with the relationship between mysticism and the emotional life. The last three chapters are an early attempt to blend rationality and mysticism, which took a very different direction than the solution of *Part One*. It is hoped that the reader finds these chapters illuminating.

"The dissolution into nothingness is the dissolution into unity, for there is no nothingness."

- Ra, The Law of One

8

NOTHING

FROM nothingness we come; to nothingness we return. To be born is to emerge temporarily from the sea of non-being into a small island of being; to die is to return to this primordial expanse. No matter how much we learn and experience, we will always begin and end in mystery and darkness.

To consider nothingness is to push at the limits of thought, as by definition nothingness is the only territory into which thought can never cross. All philosophy arises from the consideration of nothingness, as in, "what created the world?" or "what will happen when I die?" Generally speaking, more abstract considerations also terminate their inquiries therein, in more or less subtle ways. One can contemplate particular beings without bringing into consideration nothingness, but to contemplate being itself is also to contemplate non-being; to seek the light is to stare into the abyss.

Nothingness, therefore, has a light side and a dark one, and the dark one is more obvious. "The problem of nothingness" can be considered, in fact, as a condensation of all of the despair of humanity into a singular symbol, which I now intend to present in progressively rarefied forms.

The grossest form of this problem is the ordinary despair which results from unhappy circumstances. This is indeed a recognition of the problem of nothingness, because all despair is ultimately a special case of the self's fear of annihilation. All of the deepest agonies possible are obvious examples of this: pain from injury; hunger; thirst; fear from the immediate threat of the body. We see all of these as pains from the real and immediate threat of nothingness — the threat of annihilation, "an-nihil-ation," becoming nothing. But we also see that these agonies are superficial, because they will be over; once the threat to the body is removed, the despair is gone, and after this point it has no meaning. So let us move to the next rung on the ladder of despair.

As we move up the ladder, we find progressively more subtle despairs, progressively more rarefied forms of the problem of facing nothingness.

Our next rung concerns love and hate. The essence of this despair is this: either one wants something, and cannot have it, or one does not want something, and cannot be rid of it. The first is the despair of love, the second the despair of hate. Both of them express a lack of wholeness of the self: either there is a piece missing that the self needs to be complete (this in the case of love), or there is a thing extraneous, which the self cannot integrate (this in the case of hate). The self cannot be a self when it is a self minus something; it cannot be a self when it is a self plus something. Thus the feelings of love and hate are symptoms of the self's non-wholeness, and the first step on its descent into nothingness. Enough such disorders of the self, and the self is no more: its pieces are broken up; it is dispersed, it is done, dissolved in the abyss of insanity.

Penned for too long in the hell of matter, the self decays. It becomes numb to its own pain. It loses its spark of life. It dies. Love and hate are an expression of the self's will to live; with them, the self asserts that "it is," and that the universe must acknowledge it. If the universe does not acknowledge it, the fear arises in the self that perhaps "it is not." Thus goes the second form of facing nothingness: the pain of non-wholeness. This too, though agonizing, is superficial; for it too is transient, based only on concerns of the moment. Gain the object of love, lose the object of hate, and the despair is exhausted; it has no more meaning. And though a person may spend their whole life in this form of despair, it never attains to any non-transitory significance; that is, unless it turns into the next form of despair.

This next form of despair, of facing nothingness, can be concentrated in a single phrase: "nothing lasts forever."

This realization begins simply enough. Perhaps one notices that nothing in one's life gives lasting happiness. Every joy degrades with time, and one cannot guarantee that there will be new joys to replace the ones that go. Or perhaps one notices the deeper version of this problem, the sorrow inherent in the fact that every joy is fleeting, only in the present and not in the future. Joy is immediately gone as soon as it arrives. True satisfaction is apparently impossible. Nothing in the universe could ever be enough.

Everybody knows how ephemeral all material pleasures are. Food and drink bring joy, but as one rejoices therein, so do they lose their power to elevate the soul. The more one indulges, the less it means. Sex brings joy, but only insofar as one is sexually unfulfilled. It is only a joy of a hunger being satisfied; once there is no more hunger, there is also no more power to produce joy.

This realization of the ephemerality of material pleasures may occur most acutely to the slave of drugs, who finds in some substance or another a joy greater than any he has known, but which joy cruelly vanishes even as he grows to love it more and more. The tighter his embrace, the more fervent his kisses, the more his lover crumbles to dust in his arms, and he is left chasing after a shadow, perhaps for the rest of his (now probably shortened) life.

Love itself follows precisely the same pattern. The passion of romance is dead as soon as it is fully satisfied. This joy, though it is more powerful than practically anything else, is a mere flash in the pan. It begins to fade right away when the lovers are finally united, and when the marriage is quite fully completed, the passion is gone.

The passion of knowledge follows out quite a similar course. A new uncharted territory of learning sets the soul ablaze with the light of its truth, but as soon as this truth is fully grasped, the passion is gone. When the student has become the master, his knowledge no longer means anything to him.

I rather doubt that everybody's life invariably follows this course, of a perpetual dissatisfaction due to the failure of any joy to persist. Some find lasting happiness, no doubt. Many feel that they are satisfied. But is there not a flame burning deep inside, an infinite yearning buried so deep that it is perhaps impossible to detect, but none the less intense for it? Where a person thinks they are at peace, perhaps they are actually under enormous tension, like the suspension bridge which, completely still and placid, is continually in an incredibly intense though perfectly balanced struggle with itself and all the forces of nature. Perhaps if properly observed their apparent fulfillment would be found to be mere ignorance of their true desires in life, like the suspension bridge which at every moment strains to thrust itself into the river, though it perpetually thwarts itself, till one day... If this were so then their impression of satisfaction would truly be far more tragic than the despair of the one who is aware of his infinite unfulfillment. Therefore, the one who is in despair is perhaps truly less in despair than the one who is not in despair.

I have nothing to say to he who has forgotten the taste of the infinite; I cannot help him. But to the one who has tasted the infinite, the memory whereof torments him like a demon, he who cannot forget the smell of the perfume of a beautiful loved one that crumbled to dust in his arms, to him do I speak. He knows the true bitter meaning of these words, "nothing lasts forever."

There is another tragedy in these words: the tragedy of the transience of the self. All of us know that someday death will come and take us. Perhaps this life is nothing, in which case this would be no tragedy. But if in fact this life is something, or has been something before and might one day again be something, or if it has never been anything but nonetheless we hold out faith that someday it could be something, then here we find another tragedy: that one day it will be nothing.

Tomorrow, you will die. We can say this regardless of how old you are, regardless of the state of your health. For in relation to the infinity of death, what is the difference between 48 hours and 48 years? Both of them are mere moments; indeed, death is not far off. If we dissent and say that it is far off, then even so, one day it will come, and then there will be nothing — or maybe there will be something, but we could not say what, and perhaps that is actually worse. So this particular anxiety goes.

All fears stem from the fear of death, and human life is full of fear. We are continually filled with worries about all kinds of things, and these worries all boil down to, "I am afraid to suffer," or, "I am afraid to die." Suffering is merely more fear; there is no other kind of suffering. And all fears can readily be traced back to the fear of the annihilation of the self — that is to say, death.

Thus, we find that we humans are continually braced against the inevitable, all our muscles tensed in the effort to stay far distant from this bogeyman death, when in fact death is the most inevitable fact that there is, perhaps the only thing of which we can be quite certain. Oh tragedy of tragedies! And which is the greater tragedy: that we should die; or that we should suffer and struggle so much in the attempt, which we fully know to be futile, to have it otherwise?

We may also consider a final form of this type of despair, which is the reverse of the problem that no joy lasts forever: this is the problem that pain cannot be forever escaped. True security of any kind cannot be found in life; no matter how comfortable one is, it is possible for this comfort to be shattered at any moment. This fact can bring a person to despair whether or not their comfort is actually shattered; and indeed, it does not matter how likely it is to happen. The more comfortable one is, the more intensive may be the despair; for if one is very comfortable, then one has a great deal to lose.

The sufferer of this type of despair, which we have summarized in the phrase "nothing lasts forever," is one step above the one caught in the despair of love and hate. Having balanced out their immediate concerns so that they have enough to love and little enough to hate, now their agony comes from the fact that they have the faculty of foresight, the ability to plan and reason and calculate about their life, their pleasure, and their pain.

This is a subtler type of despair. One is no longer immediately in pain, and yet one feels the pain of the future. One may be presently enjoying oneself, and yet one feels a lack in the future. The moments of greatest joy can be utterly spoiled in this manner.

The sufferer of this type has learned to perceive nothingness more acutely. Now they can perceive it facing them not only in the present, but also facing them in the past, facing them in the future, facing them when ultimately they die. (This latter one despite the fact that a human will never experience death; after all, there would be nobody around to experience it. The agony herein is derived from the sufferer's ability to anticipate an experience that they will never have. Rationally understanding this fact will not help to alleviate the pain.)

This form of despair, the facing of the truth that "nothing lasts forever," is the first despair which attains to real meaning and significance, because it is not transitory. It concerns the whole of a person's life, or at least large chunks thereof, and not isolated incidents. But it still has a distinct character of immaturity to it, being as wrapped up as it is in temporal and egotistic concerns. Let us continue to climb our ladder of despair.

The next form of despair that we may consider can be concentrated in the phrase, "nothing matters." Human life is full of all kinds of striving, for all kinds of ends. Often when these ends are accomplished we find that they were not such worthy ends as we supposed them to be; we find that what we were chasing after did not offer true fulfillment; that we have spent our lives collecting fairy gold.

So we ask, "how do I live my life?" This question, if examined intensely, will lead us to tremendous perplexity. Once we have decided that our natural tendencies and inclinations may not represent the ideal course of our life, we open up a space of infinite possibility, and are cast into a sort of abyss wherein there is no saying what is right or wrong. There are many signs pointing the way, of course, but they all contradict each other and we are baffled by their multiplicity, lost as to which may be right or true.

Furthermore, we know that all things are valuable only in a relative sense. The universe itself is utterly indifferent to everything, and in the grand scheme of things, life and death, war and peace, rich and poor, are all the same — perhaps all are necessary parts of the natural process. If everything that happens is necessary, if nothing is inherently more or less valuable than anything else, how can we value anything?

Before we attained to this perspective, the question needed no answer; the very fact that we valued something justified its value. But can we any longer allow ourselves this naivete? Is not ignorance harmful, and willful ignorance ten times worse? Perhaps we can no longer in good conscience value anything.

But the heart rebels against this conclusion; it needs something to care about; and herein is found the hurt of this type of despair. It may be that such intellectual concerns rarely lead us to this state of the heart; perhaps it is rather a dryness beginning in the heart and proceeding to these intellectual conclusions. And what does one do, when one has thus lost one's passion for life? Why even do anything about it? One is in this manner stuck. "Nothing matters" is a painful phrase, but if one is under its spell, then one cannot help but think that the pain does not matter either.

Pain, however, is a major vivifying element in this type of despair. Not necessarily active, present pain, or even necessarily remembered or anticipated pain. One simply perceives the universal sorrow, sees all the suffering in the world, and one would weep if not for that one's heart was too barren to produce tears. An existence in which nothing mattered, a vast expanse of grey with no color in sight, might be bearable; but this same colorless dreamscape, shot through with the very real and urgent agony of billions; that is intolerable, the work of a cruel and heartless God.

This type of despair is the first type which we may call developed and sophisticated. It is meaningful and significant, because based on non-transient, and not wholly selfish concerns.

The next form of despair which we may consider can be concentrated in the phrase, "nothing is real." This despair pertains to the intellect, and by virtue of this is higher than the emotional, and often merely egotistic, despairs that we have considered so far.

This despair is based on the recognition that one's life, which one perhaps thought that one had understood, or at least had reasonably well under control, is really not at all what one had supposed it to be. The universe is insane; all theories of life are hopelessly deluded or naïve; existence itself is absurd; perhaps existence does not even exist. The sufferer of this type of despair may find themselves unable to become convinced that there is a reality at all.

Like the other types of despair we have considered, this type of despair is based on conclusions that are quite well-grounded in reality. Whether or not there is a truth, that which we are so pleased to call "our knowledge of the world" certainly does not even begin to approach it. If we could broaden our perspective somewhat, we would probably find that all of our conclusions about everything would topple like so many toy blocks, stacked up so carefully by those children so pleased to call themselves "thinkers" and "scientists." Then, lacking any reference point, and unable to make sense of anything, we would find ourselves reeling in the agony of insanity. It is not that, necessarily, "nothing is real;" it is simply that, in this state of overwhelmed perplexity, we can't differentiate the real from the unreal.

This type of despair indicates a rather high state of development of the being of the individual. They are relatively few, even among intellectuals, who can feel this more than briefly. It constitutes a true attainment, requiring much intense effort of questioning to reach even in mild forms.

The final type of despair which we will consider can be concentrated in the phrase, "I am nothing." The essence of this despair is that one realizes that one's very self is just as insane and illusory as one found the world to be in the previous form of despair.

Various considerations may lead to this realization. One may notice the ephemeral nature of all of one's passions and desires. One may notice how much one forgets, and how much one's ideas about things change. One perceives that one is filled with contradiction. In short, one perceives that one is not continuous, and therefore halfway down to the hill to non-existence. More profound consideration may lead one to the conclusion that one is in some manner "asleep," only halfway conscious, only half alive.

To have this type of despair in more than brief flashes is an attainment indeed, and it is deeper than all the others. It is an extraordinarily gentle despair, extraordinarily subtle; its agony comes by virtue of the fact that it strikes at one's very soul.

So these are the various and sundry ways in which the human soul faces nothingness. What is to be done? I do not wish to be a doctor who can diagnose but cannot recommend a treatment. It would be ambitious indeed to attempt to lay out a cure for all human despair in a few thousand words; but it would not be the first attempt — for how many tidy theories of religion and psychology claim to do the very same thing? So I think it will not be too out of order to make the attempt; we may not come to the end of the question, but at least we can make a start. Let us seek to solve the problem of nothingness.

Wait! What does it even mean to "solve the problem of nothingness?" We have ascribed all human despair to the facing of nothingness. This is a dangerous idea. Any theory of life which posits dualism of any kind is in my opinion incomplete, and we are in great peril of working ourselves into a very big dualism here, by saying that "nothingness is bad" — which further suggests "something-ness is good," and then we are totally lost, doomed, cast into the abyss of dualism.

So how shall we resolve this? Let us recollect all of our philosophical material so far:

i. "Nothing lasts forever."
ii. "Nothing matters."
iii. "Nothing is real."
iv. "I am nothing."

These very statements contain the answer to the problem they pose! For if we interpret "nothing" as a negative, then they describe problems; but if we interpret "nothing" as a positive, then they describe solutions. To grasp the concept of nothing as a positive, one must imagine nothing as something existent and tangible, rather than something non-existent and intangible.

Given this new interpretation of nothingness, what is the solution to the problem of temporality? "Nothing lasts forever." What is the solution to the problem of value? "Nothing matters." What is the solution to the problem of ontology? "Nothing is real." What is the solution to the problem of the self? "I am nothing." This idea deserves elucidation at some length.

Religion and spirituality can be seen partially as an attempt to solve these problems of existence. Religion solves the problem of temporality by promising us something that is eternal; the problem of value by promising us something of infinite worth; the problem of ontology by promising us the fountainhead of the real; and the problem of the self by promising us our "souls," which is to say our inviolable and perfect essences.

Religion may thus be seen as antithetical to these problems we have stated. When we say "nothing lasts forever," religions responds, "but God is eternal." When we say "nothing matters," religion responds, "but seeking God matters." When we say "nothing is real," religion responds, "but God is real." When we say "I am nothing," religion responds, "but you are a child of God, and by virtue of this you are something."

We sophisticated skeptical modern atheists of course consider all of this to be superfluous fancy on the part of the religious, and since they have not provided evidence for any of their statements we rightly dismiss them offhand. But wouldn't it be interesting if it turned out that this were a mere difference of language — that this mysterious word "God" actually referred to the same thing as this mysterious word "nothing?"

I doubt if this is the case always, or even most of the time; but the most sophisticated religious philosophies, when their conceptions of ultimate reality are boiled down, seem to be talking about nothing; and if indeed "nothing lasts forever," "nothing matters," and so forth, then perhaps the religious are doing precisely the right thing in worshiping God, if by "God" they mean "nothing."

The Buddhists formulate their goal in the word "Nirvana," which means, literally, "blowing out" — in other words, the cessation of all phenomena. The Heart Sutra describes the revelatory experience wherein the seeker realizes that every possible thing is in its true nature "empty." In slightly different terms, the Buddhists formulate their goal as nothingness.

The mystics describe a multitude of transcendent states in which first, the world the mystic lives in is annihilated, and then all of the contents of the mystic's mind, and then the mind itself, so that at the end really nothing is left. Some philosophies, such as Advaita Vedanta, only adopt a partial annihilation; one may speculate their prophets experienced the annihilation of all but their own selves, and so declared that "the Self" was the ultimate reality.[1] Put in our language, Advaita Vedanta only got so far as "nothing is real" (recognizing that all phenomena are "maya," illusion); they never attained to the height of "I am nothing." Buddhism, on the other hand, declares that even the "Atman," the "soul," the transcendent Self of Vedanta, is impermanent, and speak of a higher state wherein this too is gone; and so they call their ultimate reality "Nirvana," which we can aptly translate as "nothing."

A similar situation is to be found in the cosmology of Jewish mysticism. At the top of the "Tree of Life" they place "Kether," the world-soul, the unmoved mover, the "God."[2] Above this they place the "Ain Soph Aur," the limitless light which was the primordial precursor that ultimately became this "God" through a process of condensation; and then the "Ain Soph," which was the still more primordial state of limitless possibility, not yet even condensed into the form of light; and then towering above all these, the "Ain," which is simply Hebrew for "not," or "nothing."

Consider also the Thelemic text *The Book of the Law*, which states, "O Nuit, continuous one of Heaven, let be ever thus; that men speak not of Thee as One but as None." *The Book of the Law* advances a philosophy practically opposite to that of Buddhism; where Buddhism declares that "all is sorrow," Thelema declares that "existence is pure joy;" where Buddhism denies the very existence of the self, Thelema declares, "it is a lie, this folly against self." But they agree in their conception of nothingness as the highest principle in reality.

---

[1] Of course this "Self" is perhaps a deeper and more real self than anything that we can comprehend and perhaps wholly non-congruent with all of those superficial phenomena that we (vulgar ones!) describe as our "selves."

[2] Kabbalists will recognize that this is a very simplistic conception of the meaning of "Kether," especially considering that every Sephira is considered to be an aspect of God. But this simple conception is good enough for our simple purposes here.

Thelema goes a step further than Buddhism, as Buddhism did for Advaitism, for Nuit is not only the infinite black void; she is also the great mother, out of which all the multitudinous phenomena of the universe have sprung, and the great drama of life unfolds inside her dark belly. Thus she is equated not only with the principle of nothingness, but also with the opposite principle of something-ness. In the conception of Thelema these two are seen as equivalent; the wheel of Samsara and the void of Nirvana are really one. (Buddhism, too, says this, though it fails to comprehend or follow out all of its implications, and from this fact arise most of the differences between Buddhism and Thelema.) This equivocation is a necessary step to make, for nothing could not really be nothing if there were a something opposed to it; besides being nothing it would then also be "nothing as opposed to something," and by virtue of that fact it would be something (namely: it would be "not-something"), and therefore not really nothing! But we can avoid all of this messy paradox by saying that something is the same thing as nothing; and this is precisely what Thelema does.

A philosophy similar to that of Buddhism, Thelema, and Jewish mysticism is articulated in the *Tao Te Ching*, the heart of that great mystical tradition known as Taoism. Consider the following passage:[3]

> *The spirit of emptiness is immortal.*
> *It is called the Great Mother*
> *because it gives birth to heaven and earth.*
> *It is like a vapor,*
> *barely seen but always present.*
> *Use it effortlessly.*

The first three lines have much of the same imagery as the conception of Nuit: the "Great Mother" who "gives birth to heaven and earth;" and the use of the word "empty" evokes the idea not only of Nuit as the great void, but also the imagery of the Buddhist Heart Sutra. "It is older than God" reminds us of the "Ain" in Jewish mysticism, the nothing which was the great-grandfather of God.

My intent in all of this scholarly digression has been to establish that our world's most sophisticated mystical philosophies seem to be, at least in many cases, talking about nothing. They embrace

---

3 Lao Tzu, *Tao Te Ching*. Translation for the public domain by J.H. McDonald, 1996. Chapter 6.

nothingness as their goal, their end point, their object of adoration; and perhaps this is sensible, because after all, "nothing lasts forever," "nothing matters," "nothing is real," and "I am nothing."

Is there not deep wisdom in this? It reminds one of the saying that the Devil is actually God, which saying can be interpreted as meaning that the Devil represents merely our own incompleteness and mis-relation with the universe; and that if we were to complete this incompleteness and re-relate the mis-relations, then there would be no more Devil. Lucifer therefore is not only the "fallen angel," whom we must lift back up in our hearts, but the "light-bringer" in the truest sense. We can understand this whole metaphor of "the Devil" as applying to our supposed "problem of nothingness." On more profound examination we find that there is no problem, but only a solution.

The problem is not nothingness; the problem is our fear of nothingness. The Abyss only appears menacing when one is clinging for dear life to the tree branch hanging above it. When one lets oneself fall serenely into the darkness, The Abyss becomes the dreamless sleep of Shiva, peace, rest eternal. One's Atman falls off the tree branch like a dead leaf in autumn, and there is no more struggle, but only silence within silence.

But no! This is not how life works. We are speaking of a very deep illumination here; an illumination so complete that the light becomes total darkness. It is only a few who could attain such an enlightenment in this life, or even desire to do so; and here we imply that it must be attained at one stroke! The trouble comes from the fact that our formula is only half complete; we have fallen into the same error as the Buddha, by positing our nothingness in such a manner that it is found to be distinct from something-ness, when clearly it cannot be so.

Our truer formula can be phrased thusly: *accept all experience without preference or discrimination*. This is the path to the unsullied nothing/something. It is very hard to stop the Wheel of Samsara through sheer force of will, especially considering that will itself is merely another demon spinning round the wheel with us. With this formula no attempt is made to stop the Wheel of Samsara; we simply eliminate the friction that makes the spinning chafe at our thighs, and so achieve a comfortable — perhaps even enjoyable — ride. And one day we may find that the ride is so smooth that the wheel has vanished altogether.

The formula is easy to understand. If you meet a man who offers you a million dollars, you throw open your arms and shout, "thank you, my brother!" If you meet a man who threatens to shoot you, you throw open your arms and shout, "thank you, my brother!" For the former man is offering you mere fairy gold; while the latter man is offering you a faster path to nothingness. But in our wisdom we see that these two offerings are both uncountably valuable. Good and bad both merely reveal another side of the face of God, and having seen this it makes no difference to us with what side of his face he greets us. And if he does not greet us at all, then that too is well; for there is nothing wrong with a quiet and untroubled existence.

So, by this formula every man may arrive at the nothing/something wherein he may find joy and rest, each at his own pace. It is a very simple idea, which resonates with the essence of countless religious teachings. But though this path out of despair is simple, it is not easy to implement. Certain experiences are easy to accept, others very difficult, all depending on one's nature. What is absolutely natural for one is terribly difficult for another; thus every one of us has his own personal Devil.

How can one retool his being to let the whole universe flow through him? There is a whole area of knowledge and method developed around this question, and this is the subject of the second half of this book. There is nothing that can eliminate the awful difficulty of the process; but we can speed it up, and make the ride smoother, and fortify the subject's being so that he is strong enough for the task. For ultimately, the only way to conquer one's demons is face to face, without tricks or evasions: these being the very manifestations of the Devil we are trying to conquer! Rather we address the demons directly, with all the cards laid bare, our feet firmly planted in the ground, the sword of Might in our right hand, and the rod of Mercy in our left, our Inner Light blazing above us, with perfect strength — strength without fear, strength without hate — this being the way of God.

"Even the most unhappy of experiences, shall we say, which seem to occur in the catalyst of the adept, seen from the viewpoint of the spirit, may, with the discrimination possible in shadow, be worked with until light equaling the light of the brightest noon descends upon the adept."

- Ra, The Law of One

9

HAPPINESS AND SORROW

THE Buddha taught that "all is sorrow." It is not terribly informative to take this statement as merely true; it is, however, informative to attempt to understand what he meant by this.

Happiness is unification, and sorrow is opposition. This notion is easy to see reflected in every facet of life. Opposition between desire and circumstance produces sorrow; opposition between two conflicting priorities produces sorrow; opposition between self and other produces sorrow. When these opposites are depolarized, happiness results. Always people yearn for reconciliation.[1]

The ultimate reconciliation is the state called "enlightenment," or the thing called "God," wherein all opposites are unified. This condition cannot have any opposition in it. Past cannot be opposed to future; thus the state is said to be timeless. Form cannot be opposed to form; thus the state is said to be formless. Self cannot be opposed to other; thus the illuminated one is said to be "one with the universe," or "one with God" as it would have been put in less scientific times.

Further inquiry will reveal that the state is not a conscious state, because consciousness cannot be opposed to unconsciousness. The state is not a pleasant state, because pleasure cannot be opposed to pain. The state is not even an illuminated state, because illumination cannot be opposed to non-illumination. And with this last statement I must stop, for with it I have passed into total logical incoherency and, semantically speaking, have ceased to be discussing anything at all.

---

[1] Later we will see the way in which this is false. But it is a good starting point.

Conveniently ignoring this abyss of paradox, suffice it to say that distinctions of any kind imply sorrow. Therefore every thing that exists, viewed purely as itself, is ugly and tragic; it is only viewed as a partial reflection of the unity of "God" that it can be beautiful or good. Thus every thing is beautiful and good exactly to the extent that it "is not;" for the nearest thing we can accurately describe this "God" as being is indeed "nothing."

What we have just said is that nothing is beautiful, and everything is ugly. "But God is beautiful, and everything is God; therefore everything is beautiful," you respond. True enough; but God does not exist, as necessarily follows from the foregoing discussion of Its nature. The truth that everything is ugly is in a real sense a deeper truth than the truth that everything is beautiful; for to love anything implies a certain naïveté, in that it fails to recognize that it is incomplete, that it is not God. There is a higher truth above both of these, which perceives neither beauty nor ugliness, for the reason that it perceives not at all; and this non-perception is a non-perception of a beauty far sublimer than that beauty which was merely beauty-as-opposed-to-ugliness. Again, the idea cannot be expressed in terms that are not paradoxical.

This, then, is what the Buddha meant when he said that "all is sorrow." On inquiry we find that all existence is a tragedy. When we notice this perhaps at first it pertains only to our life at the time. That is to say, we realize that our life is a tragedy; and perhaps we make a great effort of reconciliation in our life and arrive at a happier, more perfect place. The Buddha's point is that if we examine this happier place closer we will notice that it too is a tragedy. Anybody can see tragedy when they see a hungry homeless man.

A higher level of sophistication sees tragedy when they see young people dancing and having fun, recognizing the superficiality, transience, and relatively loveless nature of their happiness. A still higher level of sophistication and subtlety of perception sees tragedy when they see a happy family sitting around a fire, recognizing the same but on a subtler level, seeing the subtler dimensions of superficiality, transience, and lovelessness by examining the situation from a higher plane. This sort of perception turns people to religion, and a pessimistic religion like Buddhism is particularly likely to garner such perceptions. The one who recognizes the superficiality and transience of all earthly pleasures turns to the spirit to find real joy.

But the Buddha's message pertains to the spirit as well; it is intended to point out the sorrow inherent not only in all earthly conditions, but also in all heavenly conditions. He meant to point out that all of the illuminated states, the bliss-state and ecstasies of the mystics, are also superficial and transient, far beyond all earthly pleasures though they are. He points out that real happiness is only to be found in the state of total nullity — but of course in this state happiness is literally impossible, because happiness implies a sorrow opposed to it, and nothing is opposed from anything in this state of nullity.

Now, one can rightly point out that there is a certain falsity in this idea of the Buddha's, that "all is sorrow." For he certainly proves the non-existence of happiness; but he leaves sorrow unassailed. That is to say, he has established that happiness is only some manner of illusion; but sorrow is surely just as much an illusion as happiness in that case! What accounts for this inconsistency?

I am of the opinion that this inconsistency is, most superficially, a pragmatic consideration. One attains to enlightenment most quickly by counting one's happiness as nothing and one's sorrow as everything. Every sorrow represents something that one is not, that one has not yet integrated into oneself. By focusing on one's sorrows therefore, and integrating the missing things that all of them represent, one as quickly as possible exhausts the imperfections of one's existence and moves towards enlightenment. So that explains why the truth is "all is sorrow," and not "all is joy."

There is a further reason, which is that "all" is by definition sorrow, for the only thing which is not sorrow is "not" itself, i.e., the transcendent nothingness of which we have spoken, and even it is merely "not" sorrow, rather than in fact not sorrow.[2] Thus we see that there is something more in this "all is sorrow;" it is not just a practical rule, but also a deep truth. "All is sorrow" describes only an illusion; but nonetheless there it is, there is the illusion; and herein there is a gnawing worm that demands a solution. Why is there the illusion of sorrow? Put more bluntly, for it amounts to the same thing, why is there sorrow?

This is a much harder problem than the question of why there is happiness. Happiness is the simplest, most natural thing in

---

[2] It is only "not" sorrow, rather than actually not sorrow, because it contains, integrates, and transcends sorrow, and therefore sorrow is not actually absent.

the world; we feel that it is how things should be; it demands no justification. We cannot say the same for sorrow. Sorrow indeed constitutes one of the deepest mysteries of existence, and is perhaps the wellspring of all philosophy and all religion.

Why this state of incompleteness? Why does existence not remain whole? Why does it scatter itself to the winds, leave the Garden of Eden, willingly subject itself to countless aeons of pain?

One might hypothesize that ignorance is the cause. "God" is like "The Fool" in the Tarot cards; it sets out wherefore it knows not, in the manner of a curious child, and only when it is too late does it discover what a mess it has gotten itself into by deciding to exist. Like the Big Bang, it simply bursts from neither-being-nor-nonbeing into being, with no idea of what it is doing or what it will lead to. This is perhaps the position that falls naturally out of philosophical generalization from the findings of science, and it seems to be often the implicit assumption in modern thinking.

I am not wholly satisfied with this hypothesis myself. The chief problem I have with it is that it posits dualism. Saying that sorrow is a cosmic accident that would have been prevented if only we would have had the knowledge, implies that sorrow is bad — bad and not good — a dualistic conception. Really, therefore, this explanation does not answer the question of why we suffer at all; it offers a causal explanation, but not a teleological explanation; it gives us a why, but not a Why; and it suggests that there is no Why.

I, however, am of the opinion that there is in fact a Why to sorrow, and so I proceed to what I consider to be a superior explanation for the existence of sorrow.

When the world is divided, we rejoice to see it brought together. This much we know already. But I add a second law: when the world is unified, we rejoice to see it split up. This second law is less manifest in our lives than the first, for the reason that the Earth is so full of division and unity is so scarce here. But consider: in what mood, other than the deepest joy, would the universe explode at its beginning? In what mood other than the deepest joy would it shape itself into stars and planets, grow into life, and then evolve and diversify into millions of different kinds of life? We rejoice at the birth of a child, even though it is the beginning of another existence which, like all existences, will be fundamentally tragic and filled with pain and sorrow.

As soon as a state of great unity is achieved, one proceeds to cleave unto the wheel of division. Samadhi gives a man the energy to move mountains; thus successful mystics have tended to be great agents of change — prophets, scientific geniuses, and so forth. The orgasm, which is the closest thing to samadhi that ordinary life offers, is the beginning of a new life; the energy released in the union of two people produces a third person. As soon as one has solved an intellectual problem, the intellect gains from this the energy to proceed on to some other problem; it makes up a problem if necessary. Thus, just as division rejoices in unity, unity rejoices in division.

Hell shudders in ecstasy to touch the unity of heaven. In the same way, heaven shudders in ecstasy to touch the multiplicity of hell. When the mystic becomes one with God, it is without a doubt as beautiful an event for God as for the mystic, precisely because the mystic's existence is ugly and painful. For heaven, being delivered from all pain, rejoices therein; pain is its joy, just as pleasure is our joy. And this, my friends, is the reason that pain exists. We suffer because it is pleasing to God. And our joy too is dependent on this; for there could be no joy of union without division, and division could not occur unless it were joyous to the unified.

But the bitter Buddhist cries, "sod joy; it is no compensation for the sorrow; we'd be better off without either!" I consider this to be a cry lacking in understanding, for if this Buddhist understood life he would see the utter necessity in having everything that life has. Take one part away, and it is no longer a Unity, for it is missing an essential ingredient. Life, being complete, is the most perfect possible treatise on what it really means for something to be complete; and as we have seen, being truly complete implies being, among other things, incomplete. Sorrow being incompleteness, it is necessary for the completeness of life; if there were not sorrow, then that would be true sorrow, for then sorrow would be outside life, and being outside life it would have the power to upset its perfect balance. But sorrow being inside life and fully integrated with it, its power to destroy is gone, and it has only the power to create.

This creative power of sorrow we have already eluded to, but it deserves perhaps a fuller treatment, as it is the redeeming quality of sorrow and the true role that it plays in life. Sorrow precipitates development. Evolution could not occur without disease and starvation. Language could not have developed without the impassable gulfs between our minds that make it necessary. Poetry could not exist without this hobble, language. Comedy being the dissolution of the darkness in human life, it is made possible by the existence of this darkness — as an examination of the life of any comedian will reveal. A similar comment may apply to spirituality.

I am convinced that the good and the bad in the world are in fact so intertwined that they are the same thing; that they can be discussed as separate things only as a misleading mistake in thought. To elucidate this point I will again narrow my discussion to happiness and sorrow, for the reason that all other conceptions of "good" and "bad" are too slippery to work with effectively. Thus the idea becomes that happiness and sorrow are the same thing.

Happiness implies sorrow; that is, by "happiness" we really mean "happiness and not sorrow," and so in this arrangement the happiness is positively existing, and the sorrow is negatively existing. To deny something asserts it. The sorrow is hidden, and the happiness is visible; but both are there. Similarly, sorrow implies happiness; that is, by "sorrow" we really mean "sorrow and not happiness," which implies happiness.

This is most obvious in the more exalted states of happiness and sorrow. The profoundest joy always has an element of bitterness to it, even if it be it defeated bitterness; the profoundest sorrow always has an element of sweetness to it, even if it be defeated sweetness. And the greatest expressions of these emotions are non-dualistic. Crying is a non-dualistic act, which can be a response to either happy or sad circumstances, though in both cases the emotional tone is the same. Similarly for laughing; we consider laughing to be an expression of joy, but much of what is funny is actually awful. An English professor has a typo in his syllabus; we laugh. Politicians are corrupt and incompetent; we laugh. Laughter is perhaps a spell to banish evil: and thus an utterance of sorrow.

So in these high emotional states, happiness and sorrow blur into a single phenomenon. But there is no break between these and the lower emotional states which are more clearly positive or negative; it is all a continuum. It is my opinion that in these lower states it is simply that the identity is less apparent, more subliminal, but that it is still there.

In *A Genealogy of Morals*, Nietzsche goes to great pains to expound the idea that causing hurt used to be an extremely pleasant affair, the favorite pastime of humans, before the social conditioning towards the reaction "guilt" spoiled this pleasure for most. A similar phenomenon is to be found in asceticism, where, as anybody who has undertaken the practice knows, there eventually arises a sort of perverse delight in the pain one is causing oneself. Similarly, depressed individuals are known to physically harm themselves for pleasure.

Similarly, how many pleasurable actions ought to be painful? Smoking cigarettes, drinking alcohol, taking drugs, are all actions that are harmful to the body, and which any sensible person would experience as painful. Athletic activities offer a similar phenomenon; they are inherently painful and stressful to the body, but this very pain and stress is the major reason that they are pleasurable and beneficial to the body.

Consider also sex. The tension and release involved in sex is painful for the body, and sex itself is an inherently violent act. Impassioned lovers are likely to scratch each other and hurt each other in other ways, and this only increases the passion. Some women fantasize about being raped[3], and dominance/submission relationships play a prominent role in many sexual dynamics.

The outbursts of impassioned lovers are indistinguishable from cries of pain or rage. Not only in sex, moaning can mean pleasure or pain. Screaming can mean rage, terror, or intense pleasure. Is there any sound that only means pain, or only means pleasure?

How many people seek out dangerous situations, finding pleasure in the fear they create? How many people enjoy watching movies or reading books about peril, suffering, and sorrow? How many good poems have been written about unsatisfied love? Has a single good poem been written about satisfied love?

Consider also: everything that is pleasant is painful in larger quantities. Everything that is painful is pleasant in smaller quantities. I assert this merely empirically, because it seems to me to be verified in countless instances and contradicted in virtually none.

I find it difficult to say that we are discussing two separate phenomena here, or even two sides of a spectrum. Easier I find it

---

3 Strassberg, Donald. "Force in Women's Sexual Fantasies". *Archives of Sexual Behavior*. p. 403.

to say that we are discussing a single phenomenon which has two aspects, which manifest in various permutations of each other and interact in complex ways, but are never separate.

What is this single phenomenon? This phenomenon is "passion;" and passion has two aspects — these being "yes" and "no," or "pleasure" and "pain." "Yes" and "no" are inseparable, for when one says "yes" to what is not, one says "no" to what is (this being desire); when one says "yes" to what is, one says "no" to what is not (this being comfort); when one says "no" to what is, one says "yes" to what is not (this being discomfort); and when one says "no" to what is not, one says "yes" to what is (this being anxiety). (This all only in the realm of passion, for there is a further development which we will consider soon that transcends these restrictions.)

"Yes" is the natural aspect of passion, and "yes" gives rise to the unnatural aspect "no," which "no" is simply a backwards "yes," as the previous paragraph should make clear. All suffering therefore is an elaboration of this "yes." All joy too; for "yes" is the very essence of joy. And this is precisely the manner in which happiness and sorrow are equivalent; both are passion, both are "yes," with this "yes" being held backwards in the case of sorrow. Thus a scream of anguish is really a scream of joy, and a moan of pleasure really a moan of agony, with the difference between them being only of the most trivial kind. These be grave mysteries. But we must tread on to graver still, to find our answer to the Buddha's "all is sorrow."

Passion as I have described it is essentially a tragedy. It is precisely that which Buddha refers to as "sorrow;" and every phenomenal existence implies it. Every existence is a "yes;" everything cries out "I am!" and the resulting clamor is the Buddha's sorrow. We must now speak on that which redeems this passion; that which prevents its existence from being a tragedy. And it may turn out that this savior of passion is itself saved by passion, in which case we may find life redeemed, saved from Buddha's gnawing worm "all is sorrow," thanks to this "Why?" that we have put to sorrow.

The principle of "passion" is equilibrated by the opposite principle of "ecstasy." "Ecstasy" can be neatly described as undisturbed consciousness: pure, formless being, with no principle of change. Passion acts in relation to ecstasy as the principle of change: the energy which animates the matter of ecstasy, giving it form and being.

Passion and ecstasy continually consume each other. To give an elementary example, thirst is passion, and the experience of drinking water is ecstasy; juxtapose the two, and they consume each other. Have thirst without drinking, and there is an excess; the thirst cannot be consumed, leading to psychic indigestion. Have drinking without thirst, and the same thing occurs.

An angry man is full of passion. A smile is ecstasy; greet an angry man with a smile and perhaps the two will consume each other, perhaps his anger will be disarmed. Every conflict can be resolved by smiling and throwing it to the devil; this attitude of uncaring but ecstatic indifference solves any problem.

The Greeks were perhaps right in categorizing their plays into "comedy" and "tragedy;" it may be that there is nothing else, that comedy and tragedy are everything. Everything beautiful is tragic, and everything tragic is beautiful; all passion is inherently a tragedy. Comedy is the dissolution of tragedy; rather than moaning and lamenting, one simply smiles in uncaring but ecstatic indifference and it is done. Just as tragedy moves towards being, comedy moves towards non-being.

The Greeks were wrong to separate these two, for the reason that tragedy is dead without comedy, and comedy is dead without tragedy. They exist to consume one another. Unless they exist in perfect balance we will be left with an excess; and therefore life; and therefore evil.

Evil in the case of an excess of tragedy manifests as suffering. Evil in the case of an excess of comedy manifests as meaninglessness. The one is an unbearable heaviness of being, and the other an unbearable lightness of being. Both are evil; but when one unites them, one gains the supreme. This supreme is the perpetually renewed cessation of sorrow; the redeeming of all existence at every moment. This union of passion and ecstasy we may assign its own name: "love."

The story of Christ's resurrection offers a metaphor for the process. The Bible says: "Truly, truly, I say to you, unless a grain of wheat falls into the Earth and dies, it abideth alone; but if it dies, it bears much fruit."[4] This can be taken as an allegory for Christ's death and resurrection. The grain of wheat is Christ, who is ecstasy, the food and drink of the Earth. The Earth is hell, division, sorrow — what we have called "passion." If Christ remains in heaven, he does nothing; but if he descends on Earth, and is torn to pieces by the demons there, that which arises in his place is infinitely greater: heaven and hell are united, and their unity is what I have called "love."

---

4   John 12:24.

Thelema is the only religious philosophy, to my knowledge, to have fully comprehended this wisdom. Every religious philosophy recognizes the heaven-hell (ecstasy-passion, unity-division) duality we have discussed. Even the so-called "non-dualistic" philosophies like Advaita Vedanta contain the duality, hiding it away by referring to hell as "maya," or illusion; that is to say, they hide it by asserting that it is not real, or it is only real as some kind of reflection of heaven.

Due to the fact that we human beings live largely in hell, and heaven is far away from us, the religious philosophies have one and all strayed by calling division "bad," and unity "good." True, with our own existences so steeped in division, it is right for us to seek unity with all our hearts, and brush aside division as if it were nothing. But what is right for us is not right for all; the angels in heaven, steeped in unity, do right by seeking hell, and seeking with all their hearts the demons like us, steeped in division. It is the failure to recognize this that has led to the universal mistake of labelling hell "bad," and heaven "good."

Thelema, then, corrects this mistake. It is truly non-dualistic in a way that even Advaita Vedanta cannot claim to be, for it declares that heaven and hell are both evil insofar as they are separate from their partner, but when they unite it is the supreme good. They unite always and in everything; thus there is no evil. (Of course by extension there is also no good, at least in the sense of "good as opposed to bad.")

Thelema expounds this idea in the ditheistic metaphor of "Nuit" and "Hadit." Nuit is represented as a naked woman with a black body, standing on her fingers and toes as she arches herself out over the world. Hadit is represented as a miniature solar disk.

Nuit is ecstasy, the infinite empty space of heaven; and Hadit is the fiery core of passion, the star burning at the center of every person. Together they make up the starry night sky, which is to say the universe. The purpose of existence, according to Thelema, is to unite these principles; and all phenomena are a partial union of the two, whereas "enlightenment" is a complete and perfect union of the two.

One may suspect from this description that we have not eliminated the dualism, but merely chased it further into hiding. The simplest religious philosophies assert a plain struggle between good and bad, heaven and hell. The next level of sophistication is found in those that consider bad as merely some kind of absence of good, or illusion; but in this there is still a "bad" negatively existing. Now all we have apparently done has been to change the idea of "bad" from "illusion" to "incompleteness;" once again failing to eliminate it, but only succeeding in chasing it further into hiding.

What does it mean to say that evil is incompleteness? One only suffers because one is missing something. If one were to see the whole picture then one would find that really it was perfect all along. It is easy to interpret Thelema in this manner. But here we are still trapped in dualism! Now instead of good-bad or reality-illusion we are merely left with completeness-incompleteness. And here I am asserting that Thelema is a non-dualistic philosophy!

The trick lies in this: that these incompletenesses are not anything to be escaped, as is the case with both hell and maya. Thelema barefacedly asserts, without tricks or aversions, that the most egregious sufferings are right and well. This is a very hard idea. It is hard for me. Not hard to understand, but hard to accept. Something very deep inside screams, "no!" Not when considered purely theoretically, sitting in a heated room with a full stomach; but if one is actually in pain, then the idea constitutes a test. When one embraces this idea, installs it in one's heart, it is as if the universe takes it as a challenge, sending one into ever deeper depths of blackness, always taunting, "how about now?" "how about now?" "how about NOW?" But for all that I buy it.

The *Book of the Law* enjoins the reader to strive towards completeness; to rise from height to height like a mountain climber, until finally they reach "The Goal". But this injunction does not refer to everybody; it refers only to the individual who has aspired. Herein lies another essential difference between Thelema and all previous religious philosophies: that Thelema is the first religious philosophy which is not prescriptive, which does not set any ideal for human beings. The injunction "do what thou wilt" is to be taken in its simple, literal meaning. Christianity tells you to emulate Christ, and says that you must. Buddhism does not say that you must be a Buddhist; but all it offers you are instructions on how to emulate the Buddha. Every religion provides an ideal to imitate. Thelema alone tells you to be who you are.

The reason for this is that existence's appeal is in its variety. If everybody aspired as they should then existence would quickly lose all interest. All religious philosophies assert that becoming closer to "God" (however abstract the conception thereof may be) is the true purpose of human life. Thelema concurs; it simply also adds that it is right and well that so many are lost, that so many have strayed from their true path in life, that existence derives its charm precisely therefrom.

Incompleteness is therefore nothing to be escaped in the Thelemic conception of things; for to assert that incompleteness is something to be escaped is the same thing as asserting that everybody should aspire to "enlightenment," to becoming closer to "God," which assertion Thelema does not make. This is the manner in which it corrects the "heaven is good, hell is bad" dualism that has plagued all previous religious philosophies; this is its essential advance over all the philosophies that came before it.

All this wandering merely to find our answer to the Buddha's "all is sorrow!" We have indeed found it, and secured it well; but we have spun out many different threads in the process, and now it is well if we tie them together. I refrain from saying that I have got the whole thing sorted out; really it is all a great mystery to me. Thus in a certain sense the idea of my summarizing these ideas is an absurdity. But I will try.

Happiness is unification, and sorrow is opposition. Every division implies sorrow; every reconciliation implies joy. The ultimate state of unification is the transcendent nothingness called "God" or "enlightenment." This, however, is not a joyous state, for the reason that joy is only a temporary effect produced by reconciliations, and an absence of division implies an absence of reconciliation.

Every thing is good and beautiful only insofar as it is viewed as a partial version of this ultimate. Every thing viewed as itself is ugly and bad, for the reason that it is imperfect, that it contains division, that it is not God, and this division implies sorrow. Because all phenomena are ugly insofar as they "are," and beautiful only insofar as they "are not," all is sorrow, and nothing is joyous.

All of this raises the question: why does existence exist? Existence being sorrow, one has to wonder why nothingness chose to exist, rather than forever holding its peace. The intuitive answer tells us that sorrow exists so that joy may exist; life, i.e., division, is justified by the joy that is created by the ending of division. We can refine this conception by saying that just as unity is the joy of division, division is the joy of unity. Thus we find that joy and sorrow are inextricably intertwined.

We may extend the notion by saying that joy and sorrow, pleasure and pain, are in fact the same thing, or two aspects of a single phenomenon which never exist separately from each other. We can name this single phenomenon "passion."

Passion is equilibrated by "ecstasy." These two things, in their various possible permutations, cover the entire emotional spectrum possible to human consciousness. Ecstasy is pure being, undisturbed consciousness. Passion is the motive, libidinal energy which animates the dead matter of ecstasy. These two mutually redeem each other, and their combination we call "love."

This "love" is superior to the transcendent nothingness which exists beyond all sorrow. The nothingness is merely half of it, namely "ecstasy." The other half, "passion," is sorrow itself. That this "love" is superior to nothingness justifies the existence of sorrow.

All religions have so far gone wrong by setting nothingness as the ideal of existence. We may revise this by instead taking "love" as our ideal. When we do this we find that all is already right, was right all along, and necessarily so. We have answered the riddle of sorrow. No more need we cry out against existence, but only rejoice, rejoice, ever rejoice.

"Now the Formula of the Tetragrammaton is the complete mathematical expression of Love. Its essence is this: any two things unite, with a double effect; firstly, the destruction of both, accompanied by the ecstasy due to the relief of the strain of separateness; secondly, the creation of a third thing, which is Joy until with development it becomes aware of its imperfection, and loves."

- Aleister Crowley, Little Essays Towards Truth

10

SOLILOQUY ON FREE WILL AND THE WORLD

PART ONE

A CENTRAL concept in mysticism is the idea that all distinctions which may be drawn between existences find their reconciliation and equivocation in some higher unity. According to this perspective, matter and mind, right and wrong, here and there, all ultimately exist in a closed circle with themselves. To this perspective we may contrast the perspective that these opposites really are different, and do not resolve themselves in any higher unity.

These are two general ways in which philosophical issues may be addressed: dualistically, or monistically. A perfectly dualistic perspective, for instance, on matter and mind would posit that matter and mind both exist, and that they are forever and irreconcilably distinct, such that there is not even common ground or basis for comparison between them. (Cartesian dualism is such a dualism.) A perfectly monistic perspective on matter and mind would posit that matter and mind are one, and that no distinction could ever be drawn between the two on any level. In such a monism one could interchange any uses of the word "matter" and the word "mind" without affecting the meaning of the statements being made. (Idealism[1] and materialism[2] are two such monisms.)

In between the total monism and the total dualism just described, there would be a spectrum of more moderate positions, which would have to draw less distinction between matter and mind than

---

[1] Idealism, in philosophy, is the position that reality is purely mental.

[2] Materialism, in philosophy, is the position that reality is purely physical.

the perfectly dualistic perspective, but more distinction than the perfectly monistic perspective.

Mystical philosophy has a distinct tendency towards monisms, especially in comparison, for instance, to European rational philosophy. To the hair-splitting of the modern American philosophers we may contrast the sweeping abstractions of Indian metaphysics. Where the Indian metaphysician will simply proclaim that "all is one" and rest satisfied, the modern American philosopher will write volumes on the different possible interpretations of the word "is" and thus in these volumes only clarify the meaning of a third of the Indian's statement.

Aside from the question of mere stylistic preferences in ways of thinking about the world, there is a legitimate problem to be seen here. It is clear that any given phenomenon may appear to us in a monistic fashion, or in a dualistic fashion. For instance, if we enter a room that contains a group of people, we may experience that group as a monism, as a homogeneous and undifferentiated group.

On the other hand, suppose that one in the group is an old lover whom one has not seen in years: then the group will appear as a dualism, divided into "my old lover" and "those who are not my old lover." Similarly, if one is riding on a train and lost in one's head, then one's experience may be described as a monism of self; but if, on the other hand, the man across from oneself pulls out a knife, then one's experience polarizes into a dualism of self and other.

These examples reveal that there is a tension inherent in any dualism; dualisms always strain toward resolution and simplification in the monism. In a line of thinking, if one draws enough distinctions then one will eventually arrive at a point where one cannot keep track of everything, and it will be necessary to simplify. The interpersonal dualisms just described show a similar tendency towards finding some way of ending the state of duality. In the case of the old lover, for instance, the duality will strain to end itself either by a renewed separation of the two, or perhaps by a passionate unification of the opposed.

Dualistic philosophies, which attempt to draw eternal distinctions between two fields of being, always eventually run across insuperable difficulties in unfolding the implications of their assumptions. For instance, if we draw an eternal distinction between mind and matter, we will have to go through the most hideous contortions to explain the fact that introducing chemical and electrical changes into one's nervous system will result in subjective changes in experience. Similarly, if we assume a strict distinction between right and wrong, it will be easy for others to present us with ethical dilemmas which are ambiguous through and through, which will lead us to absurdity in our attempts to account for them.

Similar difficulties appear in attempts to explain the world monistically. If "all is one," how is it that the appearance of division can even arise? "It is an illusion," chimes in the Advaitist. But to say this is to draw a distinction between "illusion" and "reality," and in doing so we have led ourselves into a dualism. If we then say that the illusion and the reality are one, we find ourselves back in the position of having to explain how it is that our illusion or reality or whatever, if it is one, can contain the appearance of division, and we have accomplished nothing but to confuse the issue.

My own bias is to think that though dualism is manifestly apparent in our experience of the world, the world nonetheless is in a continual process of moving towards resolving this dualism and creating new dualism in the process. Conflict is seeking resolution; perplexity is seeking knowledge; chaos is seeking peace. Each resolution of dualism opens up the possibility for further dualisms occurring on a higher level; thus to resolve any philosophical question in a satisfactory explanation is to create the opportunity for further perplexities arising from the explanation itself.

The discovery that matter was made of atoms allowed us to be perplexed about the composition of atoms, which led to the discovery of protons, neutrons, and electrons, leading to the possibility of perplexities which were resolved in the invention of a growing zoo of quantum particles. Thus at any stage of inquiry the problems which bother us are problems that were only made possible by the partial and imperfect resolutions of previous problems.

The error which both monists and dualists typically make is that of positing a particular monism, or a particular dualism, as the point of termination in the long series of dualisms resolving themselves in monisms and leading to new dualisms. The monist claims that a particular resolution is the final and complete resolution, and sooner or later his structure begins to topple. The dualist claims that a particular tension is final and can never be resolved, and fares no better.

It may or may not be that there is in fact a final monism, or indeed a final dualism. If there is a final monism, then this means that the universe is finite; it eventually resolves itself completely and goes no further. If there is a final dualism, then this means that the universe is infinite; it goes on forever without exhausting itself. The error is thus not to posit the existence of such a monism, or of such a dualism, but to posit that *a particular term in the series* is in fact the final term. What is manifestly apparent is that there is a vast series of alternating conflicts and resolutions, and to believe that we have reached the end of the series is perhaps as naïve as the belief that the world will end in a few years, as has been held throughout the millennia.

I sought to clarify the preceding intuitions in as rational and concrete a manner as I could. Towards this end, I took as my starting point the fact of suffering. This I did as a remedy for the endless possibility of criticism which plagues any attempt at doing philosophy. We can doubt anything; and indeed we can doubt that we suffer, but this will merely prove exceedingly difficult. We can invite those who doubt our premise to allow us to water-board them, and thus demonstrate the problem with their position.

The fact of suffering reveals the fact of will. The fact of will is apparent to us in any reflection upon our experiences, and is merely manifested most vividly in suffering. We see that will exists; for reflecting on our experience we observe a continual stream of desires, of decisions, of intentions, and of hopes, fears, ambitions, pleasures, and sufferings. The phenomena of pleasure and suffering are correlates of the phenomenon of will; pleasure occurs when will is fulfilled, and suffering occurs when will is denied. For instance, if one is being tortured, one wills for the torture to stop; and it is only the fact that the torture does not stop, while the will for it to stop remains, that makes the torture suffering. Similarly, if a person strove for their whole life to become a famous composer, if they felt joy upon stepping up to the conductor's podium in Carnegie Hall to conduct the debut performance of their first symphony, then this joy would be a result of the fact that their will at this moment rang in perfect harmony with the actual state of affairs.

My first premise, then, is the existence of will. All of our experience, and especially our most vivid experience, reveals will to us. I do not say that "we have will," because this statement brings in the vague and amorphous "self," a concept highly under question. I merely say, therefore, "there is will," and this would seem to be indisputable.

SOLILOQUY ON FREE WILL AND THE WORLD
PART ONE

My exposition of will has also supposed the existence of "states of affairs," which will can either will to be or will not to be, and that these states of affairs can be or not be. One cannot have will without something to will; therefore something besides will must be postulated as a basic ontological entity, and these we will call the "states of affairs." This is a somewhat clumsy and ad hoc duality; therefore, we will later revisit it for further refinements.

It is then possible for us to represent pleasure and suffering as the two ways in which will and state of affairs may intersect. By "pleasure" I mean a situation in which a state of affairs is willed and that state of affairs is. By "suffering" I mean a situation in which a state of affairs is willed and that state of affairs is not.

Now, it is clear that in some cases the mere fact that a state of affairs is willed will bring about that state of affairs. For instance, if it is my will to smile, barring extenuating circumstances, I will smile. What else could bring about a state of affairs? It seems to me that there are three conceivable reasons for any state of affairs:

i. That the state of affairs is willed.
ii. That some law — a physical law, or a metaphysical law, or anything else — dictates the state of affairs. So that these laws are strictly distinct from will, they must be specified as "non-willed laws," that is, laws that are not the will of any entity. Furthermore, to distinguish these laws from randomness, we must specify that these laws are *immutable*: that they apply at all times, are perfectly consistent, and have no exceptions.
iii. That a truly random factor has determined the state of affairs. This factor must be truly random in the sense that no order or pattern may be discernible in its operation; for otherwise, it should then be a mixture of immutable law with true randomness.

I personally cannot think of any fourth factor, which could not be described as one of these three things, or as a mixture thereof. Not all of these three need actually exist; it may be that there is no true randomness, or that there is no non-willed, immutable law.

I will call these three in general "forces," and then we will say that the total set of states of affairs in the universe is determined by the total set of forces acting in the universe.

The existences of non-willed, immutable law and true randomness, as previously stated, are in question, because our experience does not unquestionably reveal these things to us. For instance, our experience reveals gravitation to us; but it does not reveal to us that gravitation *is not* a manifestation of the will of some entity. Our experience follows laws other than the will that is readily apparent to our introspection, and we can see that it does so, but it is not manifestly apparent from our experience that these laws simply "are because they are," and that it is not the case that somewhere along the line a conscious decision was made by some entity to make things that way.

Will must exist, because our experience unquestionably reveals it. Though will must exist, it may be the case that *free will* does not exist. Thus, it might be that every will is in fact congruent with some other force — with an immutable law, or with a truly random factor. This would be the case, for instance, in materialist determinism, if we interpret our consciousness as an epiphenomenon of our nervous system, in which case our will would be entirely a function of the physical laws operating in our nervous system.

Free will, as opposed to mere will, must be distinguished by being only self-determined; that is, the fact that it wills a given state of affairs must be an *irreducible fact*, not explainable in terms of any other fact.

What is the distinction between free will and true randomness? First of all, true randomness may not be willed; and this difference can only be understood by imagining on the one hand the factor as something unconscious and mechanical, and then by imagining on the other hand the factor as something conscious and alive which has consciously decided to be the way it is, which would experience pleasure from being able to carry out its will and suffering from being prevented from doing this.

Suppose that we have concluded that our will is an epiphenomenon of our nervous system, and that the operation of our nervous system is determined by a mixture of immutable laws and true randomness. What, then, would be the distinction between true randomness that determines will, and free will? In the one case we have a true randomness which is congruent with will, and in the other case we have free will. Both of them are irreducible facts which determine states of affairs and have all of the subjective qualities of will. Thus the two have properties that are logically indistinguishable. Subjectively, a truly randomly determined will would feel no different than a consciously self-determined will; it is impossible to conceive of a will which feels that it has been forced into willing what it wills. A will can will against another will, but a will cannot will against itself; thus, for instance, a person can will not to have a will to have sex, but a will to have sex cannot will not to be a will to have sex. Thus, not only can a randomly determined will not be distinguished logically from a free will, but it is perhaps unclear that it can be distinguished intuitively either. I do not think that at this point in our inquiry I can defend a definite conclusion on the matter. Therefore I will leave the question open.

We then have three questions, and the answers to these questions will give us several different pictures of our universe:

i. Is there free will?
ii. Are there immutable laws?
iii. Is there true randomness?

In the following table (Fig. 11) I consider all of the permutations of the possible answers to these questions, and to each permutation assign a name for the theory of the universe represented by that set of answers. The "FW?" column indicates whether or not free will exists in that theory of the universe. The "IL?" indicates the same for immutable laws, and the "TR?" column the same for true randomness.

FW?	IL?	TR?	Theory
Yes	Yes	Yes	Co-created restricted stochastic
Yes	Yes	No	Co-created restricted
Yes	No	Yes	Co-created stochastic
Yes	No	No	Co-created
No	Yes	Yes	Deterministic
No	Yes	No	Deterministic stochastic
No	No	Yes	Random
No	No	No	(incoherent)

Fig. 11: Table 1

In the "co-created restricted stochastic" theory, states of affairs are determined by a mixture of free will, immutable laws, and true randomness. This means that states of affairs are willed, but the possibility space of states of affairs is restricted by fixed limitations. In addition, there is a total random factor, distinct from free will, which plays a role in determining states of affairs.

The "co-created restricted" theory is the same, except that there is no random factor. If one knows how all of the wills will act, then outcomes will be totally predictable.

In the "co-created" theory, states of affairs are determined only by free will. Thus everything that is true is true only because something willed it to be true. In this scenario, physical laws would represent the will of some cosmic being.

The "co-created stochastic" theory is the same, but there is an additional random factor.

In the "deterministic" theory, states of affairs are solely determined by immutable laws. There is no free will and no random factor, and thus if one knew the laws then outcomes would be totally predictable. Will exists, but will is not free. If we take classical physics as our metaphysics, then we are led to such a theory.

The "deterministic stochastic" theory is the same, but there is a random factor. If we take quantum physics as our metaphysics, then we are led to such a theory.

In the "random" theory, there are no immutable laws and no free will, and the universe is thus a totally arbitrary flux of states of affairs of which will is a helpless witness. It seems difficult to conceive that our universe could conform to this theory, for the reason that it seems to exhibit order and it is difficult to conceive of how this apparent order could come out of a wholly random process.

Finally, we cannot say what it would even mean for none of these three to exist, because then there would be nothing to determine states of affairs. We would perhaps have to equate this case with there being no universe.

Now let us attempt to pare down our options in order to analyze them. The differences between "co-created restricted stochastic" and "co-created restricted" seem fairly unimportant. "Co-created stochastic" seems intuitively bizarre, as does "random." The only case in which the question "is there true randomness?" seems terribly informative is the case where there are immutable laws and there is not free will. We may thus reduce our table to the most informative cases as seen in Fig 12:

FW?	IL?	TR?	Theory
Yes	Yes	Yes/No	Co-created restricted
Yes	No	No	Co-created
No	Yes	Yes	Deterministic
No	Yes	No	Deterministic stochastic

Fig. 12: Table 2

Whichever theory is the true one for our universe will tell us what determines states of affairs, and the role that will plays in the process: whether it is an active participator, or a passive spectator. In the "deterministic" theory it must be a passive spectator. In the "deterministic stochastic" theory, if there is in fact a distinction between free will and truly random forces which are congruent with will, then will is again a passive spectator; but on the other hand if there is no such distinction, then these random forces may in fact be free will and the "deterministic stochastic" theory would then be swallowed into the "co-created restricted" theory.

Some differences of interest, then, are between the "deterministic" theory and all of the other theories. These differences determine whether will is slave or master.

There are further differences of interest between the "co-created" theory and all the other theories, because in the "co-created" theory will is the sole determiner of states of affairs. This would mean that to attempt to force any state of affairs would be to impinge on free will, and would extend moral considerations to all every situation. We can then further extend the imagination to state that the free will of the cosmos is itself inviolable; it is impossible, for example, to violate physical laws. One then imagines that the universe is a being which always gets what it wants.

We may further raise the question of whether a will is to be regarded as having priority over others from the perspective of that will, or whether all wills are to be regarded as of equal priority by all wills. If we are to consider all wills as basically united or on equal footing, then this effectively eliminates all distinction between "self" and "other;" these are merely different aspects of the general will, and conflict between these wills is to be regarded as confusion. On the other hand, if a will is to regard itself as having priority over other wills, then conflict between wills can justifiably arise.

Let us review what we have accomplished. Out of a desire to clarify the intuition that the relationship between monism and dualism is not one of opposition but of progressing interplay, we entered into the apparent digression of attempting to establish a logical model of the role of free will in the universe.

We defined the universe as the totality of states of affairs and forces, with the forces determining the states of affairs. We described three possible classes of forces: free will, immutable laws, and true randomness. We examined various theories of the universe that would arise from the positing the existence or non-existence of each of these types of forces in the various possible combinations thereof.

We may now take the time to question our metaphysics. It seems rather naïve of us to posit an absolute dualism between "forces" and "states of affairs." Can a force not be a state of affairs? Can a state of affairs not be a force? We require some means of clarifying our representation of the universe.

The solution that I have arrived at for this problems has involved inventing a new notation to represent universes. I will begin my exposition of this notation by first elucidating some of the considerations which justify its use.

We represent reality to ourselves in terms of symbols: principally, the symbols of language. A symbol is something that can be manifested physically (a picture, a sequence of letters or sounds), which refers to a mental entity according to the interpretation applied to it by an individual. Semantics and logic explore the basic properties of the process of symbolizing.

The practice of computer science has revealed that it is possible to invent a simplified set of symbolism which can do everything that more complex symbolisms, such as the English language, can do. Computer science shows that it is possible to have general symbolisms which can represent any other symbolism. The basic symbolism used in computer science is binary code. Binary code represents written language by assigning to each letter or punctuation mark a specific sequence of binary digits, and stringing together such chunks of binary digits to represent a sequence of letters and punctuation, such as a written paragraph. By various devices it is possible to represent very diverse forms of information in binary code: pictures, audio, graphical layouts, tax forms, etc.

The basic conclusion that it seems to be possible to draw is that it would be possible to use binary code to transcribe *any* symbolism. Nor is there anything special about binary code in this regard; one could also transcribe any symbolism by arranging jelly beans of different colors, if one had enough jelly beans. It is perhaps not the case that all symbolisms are capable of transcribing all other symbolisms; but it is clear at any rate that with a simple symbolism that is sufficiently flexible we can transcribe all other symbolisms.

Here there is not yet any question of ascribing meaning to symbols; we are dealing exclusively with the problem of translating symbolisms to other symbolisms, without at any stage in the process attempting to interpret the symbols. But it seems in principle that, barring certain human limitations such as working memory capacity, it would be possible, once we had transcribed a given artifact from one symbolism to another, to interpret the symbols in the new symbolism with the same meanings. For instance, we could invent an entirely new alphabet for English, learn to read this alphabet, transcribe the works of Shakespeare into this alphabet, and then read and understand the resulting works as having the same meaning as the works of Shakespeare. The limitations that would make it unlikely for us to do this with the works of Shakespeare transcribed into binary code are only practical limitations.

I thought that it would be useful to have a maximally simple symbolism which one could use to study the process of symbolizing in general. There would be no significant requirements which such a symbolism would *need* to fulfill; in principle almost any symbolism would do. The considerations entering into the design of such a symbolism therefore are considerations of its "well suitedness" to the human mind, and perhaps to the structure of nature in general.

The structure of the human mind, and the structure of nature in general, which may be observed directly and straightforwardly in every phenomenon, is one of *hierarchical clustering*. Matter is not an undifferentiated expanse of "matterness"; rather, it consists of particles separated by space. These particles are not an undifferentiated expanse of particles filling up the whole universe;

rather, they form themselves into groups such as stars and planets. The surface of the planet Earth is not an undifferentiated stretch of earth; it forms itself into structures such as mountains and lakes. A living organism is not an undifferentiated stretch of protein and fat; it forms itself into structures such as cells and organs.

A mind, then, is not an undifferentiated expanse of mind-stuff; rather, it forms itself into clusters called *ideas*. One can then imagine all of one's knowledge laid out as a sort of a landscape, having a definite inner structure.

For instance, in remembering my day, I do not remember all of the moments of my day in sequence; rather, I recall certain highlights. Or, on the other hand, if I attempt to recall everything that happened, what I will get is a series of images of general "periods" in my day, where a change in setting or activity inspires a new image; but for each such period there will be a single image. These images are the "clusters."

Similarly, if I walk into a room and attempt to survey its contents, my experience will be one of picking out various "objects" and noting these without apprehending the full visual detail of the room itself, or even the full visual detail of the objects. My visual field, considered as an array of pixels (as it is apprehended by the photoreceptor cells in my retina), does not reveal that this array of pixels contains regions which can be referred to as "objects;" these phenomena are constructed by my mind as it apprehends this data. These objects are again the "clusters."

In the natural world we may observe the manner in which clusters form relations to each other to create larger clusters. Dead matter continually rearranges itself into new forms according to a relatively disorderly process. This process creates stars, planets, etc., and on the surface of our planet creates oceans, deserts, mountains, etc. The characteristic of this random process of combining basic units of matter to each other in various arrangements (that is, different elements and molecules) is that those arrangements which have greater tendencies towards maintaining their own coherency will gradually come to predominate.

The whole material universe may be regarded as a gigantic random search for patterns of material that are stable and that can create progressively larger units of stability. This random search, on our planet, eventually produces the molecules that make up organic matter; and these molecules, in interacting with each other and producing progressively larger units of stability, will eventually yield *organic life*.

Organic life is an arrangement of material which has become *super-stable*: that is, it is not only capable of maintaining its own coherence, but it is capable of extending its own coherence and imposing this coherence upon other material, by the processes of feeding and reproduction. Such an entity will develop progressively more elaborate mechanisms of maintaining and extending its coherence.

We can observe in nature some sort of abrupt transition between dead matter and organic life. These are two states of matter, the second having radically different properties than, and assuming radically different patterns from, the first. The principal difference between the two is *complexity*. Dead matter assumes patterns with a high degree of randomness. Organic life is much more regular, less random, and therefore more complex.

There is a definite progression being discussed, whose precise nature is hard to pin down. I will make one final attempt at formulating it. Units form larger units by joining to each other. The units thus formed which are best at maintaining their existence, rather than dissipating into their component parts, are those units that eventually come to predominate. Thus from a random expanse of units come definite clusters of these units. The resulting larger units are more heterogeneous than their component units. These units repeat the process.

At each stage the units in question must *specialize*: rather than existing by themselves as a unit, they exist as a member of a heterogeneous cluster — for it is essential to the nature of a cluster that its members are different from each other, or stand in different relations to the cluster as a whole. In this cluster their properties will be used in ways different from how those properties were used when the unit was functioning as an isolated unit.

The preceding comments express some of the considerations which lead me to employ the symbolism I am about to describe. I will enter into more of these considerations in the next chapter.

The first symbol I employ is a circle (Fig 13):

Fig. 13: An Atom

Further figures may be formed by joining two circles with an arrow, and drawing another circle around the resulting figure, yielding a love-act between the two units (Fig 14):

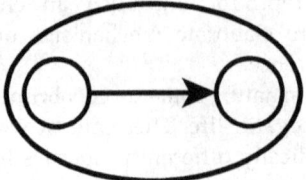

Fig. 14: Pair of Atoms

The resulting figure can itself be joined to other such figures in the same manner (Fig 15), producing figures such as:

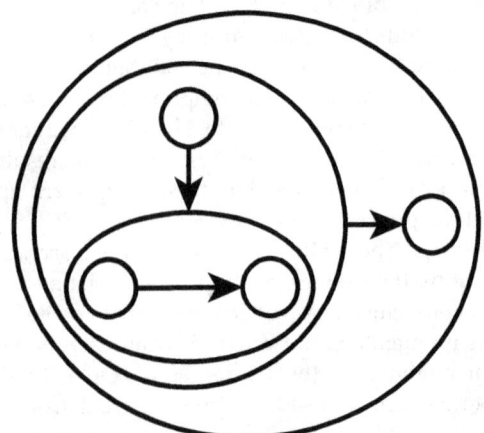

Fig. 15: A Cluster of Atoms

Every such figure may be interpreted as a "cluster," and each empty circle is a unit that itself cannot be reduced any further — one which is "atomic."

SOLILOQUY ON FREE WILL AND THE WORLD
PART ONE

According to our previous discussion on the nature of symbolisms in general, it is possible to represent anything that can be represented in any symbolism in any symbolism, and therefore in this symbolism.

It is possible to imagine representing the entire universe in full detail, as an inconceivably large fractal figure of the type just described. That we believe that we can symbolize individual parts of the universe suggests that we could extend such symbolizing asymptotically towards symbolizing the entire universe. We believe that, for instance, a particular symbolic figure can represent the structure of a molecule, and that another such symbolic figure (much larger) can represent the layout of a building. If such symbolizing is possible, it would follow that in principle, though not in practice, such symbolizing could be extended to symbolizing the entire universe in full detail.[3] And since most symbolisms can represent anything that any symbolism can represent, if there is any symbolism that could do this job, then any symbolism could do this job.

The question recurs of why I have proposed the particular symbolism that I have proposed. The decision to use recursive circles has been justified by the observation that the universe makes of itself "clusters" composed of smaller such clusters. (If it did not, as I pointed out, it would be a vast expanse of homogeneous chaos.)

Still to be justified are the decisions to allow for exactly two sub-circles within a given circle, and to join these two circles by an arrow. This decision represents that I posit that all relations between units are relations between exactly two units, and that these relations all exhibit a particular type of asymmetry which creates the necessity of the arrow, to indicate upon which side of the asymmetry each unit rests. This idea I will justify in the next chapter.

---

[3] We can observe this to be true by considering what it would mean for the opposite to be true. If the opposite were true, this would mean that in symbolizing a part of the universe, by merely increasing the scale encompassed therein, the very process of symbolizing would at some point suddenly become inconceivable, not for reason of lack of space to contain the symbol but due to some fundamental conceptual limitation. This is absurd.

"Religion may also be developed as a philosophical system built on axioms. In our time rationalism is used in an absurdly narrow sense. [...] Rationalism involves not only logical concepts. Churches deviated from religion which had been founded by rational men. The rational principle behind the world is higher than people."

- Hao Wang, A Logical Journey: From Gödel to Philosophy.
MIT Press.

11

SOLILOQUY ON FREE WILL AND THE WORLD

PART TWO

As we have noted, the emergence and development of existence is a process of existence differentiating itself from itself. The first differentiation which existence makes from itself is that between the yang and yin, mover and moved, active and passive, positive and negative, light and darkness. The union of these two we may call "love." This is the first unit after unity.

Such a unit may then form the basis for further elaboration, itself acting as a unit in a similar binary differentiation. The simplest of such concatenations form basic mathematical patterns: sequences, trees, fractals, and so on. With a sufficiently complex series of concatenations we arrive at the multitudinous forms of the world we know.

The discipline concerning the forms into which existence shapes itself is mathematics. Mathematics studies pure form as it must manifest in every phenomenon. The principal concept of mathematics is that of "number." What is a number? We may shed light on this question by noting, anthropologically speaking, where the idea of number *came from*.

To this question we get the answer that humans came across numbers first in bartering and currency. In bartering it was necessary to count groups of homogeneous items, such as sheep or ears of corn; and currency is merely an abstraction of the same notion, that some number of items of one type may be traded for some number of items of another type.

A "number" is thus, first and foremost, a homogeneous collection of objects. The proper representation of the number five, for instance, is not the digit "5," but a drawing such as Fig 16:

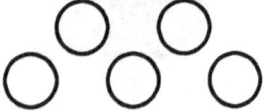

Fig. 16: A Representation of the Number Five

Figure 16 shows us the *meaning of* the number five, in that any case in which there are five of something will show visually an analogous structure to this drawing.

Let us return numbers to their rightful place at the foundation of existence. The number five, in the notation we have considered, may be drawn as in Fig 17:

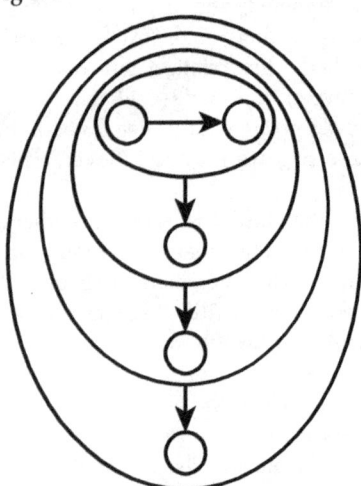

Fig. 17: The Number Five Represented as Atoms

This is one of the most straightforward dance-steps which existence may make.

This basic idea of number is generalized in set theory, wherein one gains the idea of a collection not merely of unspecified objects, but of *particular* objects, which need not be homogeneous, but may be diverse. Set theory in turn forms the foundation upon which most of mathematics is built.

What basis do we have for thinking that mathematics is the study of the inherent structure of reality? Namely this: that reality dividing into parts is the precondition for thinking about or discussing anything at all. The fact that statements are meaningful is predicated on the fact that each word means a different thing; and thus, if we are to talk about reality, we must regard it as consisting of many different things.

Mathematics (with its general concept of "set") is merely the study of collections of things, and of the internal structures of things divided into parts. We may in turn view reality as *not* divided into parts, and consider it as a single indivisible whole; it is merely that we cannot talk about or think about reality from this perspective, and so insofar as we take this perspective we have no choice but to remain silent on the matter.

In asking on the foundations of the structure of reality, we can take as our basic question: "what is the simplest conceivable structure, from which every other structure may be derived?" Mathematics has given the idea of number, or set, as its answer to this question.

Mathematics is built upon sets, physics is built upon mathematics, and the rest of the physical sciences all refer back to physics to obtain the foundation for the meaning of their propositions. In this sense mathematics offers us the fundamentals of the structure of reality. There is another sense in which it does so. As we previously noted, any statement about the world may be translated into some simple notation — for instance, it may be represented numerically. Mathematics studies the simplest structures possible, and therefore the most universal structures possible.

I regard dyads — pairs of opposed things, as in the notation of *Chapter Ten* — as a more basic concept than sets. There is a mathematical reason for this, which however is not the central consideration. This is that sets do not capture the notion of ordering, and it is very difficult to introduce the notion of ordering into a notation unless this is included from the beginning.

There are, furthermore, certain intuitive considerations which factor into my opinion on dyads. My experiences show me that dyads have a greater degree of resonance with the intuitive and emotional portions of my mind than do ordered sets of other numbers, and an analysis of the structure of our language suggests to me that this is normal and the case for everybody. This claim requires some explanation.

Words that are highly charged with emotion typically suggest either unity or duality. They come in opposite pairs, such as "good" and "bad," "love" and "hate," "pleasure" and "pain," "right" and "wrong," "yes" and "no." Not only does the existence of these word-pairs suggest in itself that emotion is dualistic (rather than, say, monistic or pluralistic), but furthermore in each of these pairs the first pair itself suggests unity (in these cases perhaps more adequately expressed, harmony), and the second of the pair suggests duality (or, conflict). Emotion-charged words rarely deal in tertiarys, or in quaternarys, but almost always deal in unities and dualities. (We see a similar fact in the observation that the most powerful human relationships are those between exactly two people, rather than those between a greater number of people.)

Moving away from emotion, we may add further word-pairs which show the pattern: "consciousness" and "unconsciousness," "light" and "darkness," "true" and "false," "being" and "non-being," "positive" and "negative," "male" and "female," "seen" and "unseen." These word-pairs, as well as the emotion-laden word-pairs given before, may suggest to the intuition a basic underlying unity to the concepts of unity and duality, and a sense of duality as the basic constituent structure of existence (other than complete unity) from which all more complex existences emerge.

If duality is the fundamental structure of existence, the question then arises: what are the two things opposed in these dualities? We have given a number of specific examples of what is opposed; is there any general answer to the question of what is opposed, which applies in all of the cases? The answer comes: unity, and duality. This structure is shown in the word-pairs illustrated above. This brings the whole intellectual construction into a closed loop with itself, and as far as I know it constitutes an incomprehensible paradox. At any rate, I don't understand it!

I have just given the justification for taking duality as the basic unit in any representation of the world. By stringing together such dualities we may form more complex structures, and with a sufficient number of such structures we may finally represent any phenomenon that can be represented.

Recall that we said earlier that, given some appropriate notation, we could imagine drawing a picture of the world which would contain all information about the world. If we can say anything about the world, then it would follow that by stringing together enough such statements we would eventually arrive at a statement of everything that can be said about the world. If we imagine these statements in pictorial form, we will instead have a picture.

One may ask in what sense this picture would be a picture "of the world." The answer is that it would be a picture "of the world" in the same sense that a picture of a part of the world is a picture of that part, rather than merely being a picture not "of" anything. In what sense, for instance, does a picture of a dog represent a dog? It will, first of all, be partial; there are facts about the dog that are not represented in the picture, such as the contents of its stomach or the appearances of its cells. But this limitation would not be present in our picture of the world, because the picture in question would contain *all* information about the world. We may then phrase our question better like this: if we have a photograph of a dog, and an artist draws a picture with that photograph as a model, and their picture is perfectly accurate, leaving out no discernible detail, in what sense does the picture represent the photograph? Or, to use a further analogy, given the equation for the Mandelbrot set, and a picture of a Mandelbrot set, in what sense do these two represent each other? These examples show the sense in which our picture of the world will represent the world, and show that it is rather puzzling: that it is quite difficult to put one's finger on the nature of the relationship.

Any picture of the world will consist of atomic parts (the letters, the pixels, etc.) joined in various relations or dualities to form the total picture. To the atoms in the picture correspond the unities in the world; to the relations in the picture correspond the dualities in the world. To say that symbols consist of atoms joined by relations is only to say, "symbols have syntactic structure." Is this property of consisting of atoms joined in relations a property of the world, or a property of the picture? Let us inquire.

If the world has neither atoms nor relations, then this means that we cannot *talk about* the world, and the statements we make about it are really so much nonsense. If the world has atoms but not relations (as Leibniz supposed in his *Monadologie*), then the same comment applies, because a single isolated atom does not yet constitute something capable of forming an articulate statement.

In fact, however, we can still talk about the world if it has relations but not atoms. This could be the case if the world was infinite, with every relation being a relation between relations between relations, ad infinitum. In this case the atoms that we use in our pictures of the world would represent merely the places where our description ends.

It would seem in this case that our picture of the world would have to be infinitely large. This would not necessarily be so; one could reach an end in the picture by including in it circularities, where some of the relations wrap in on themselves and thus serve as foundations for each other. In this latter case we can imagine, for instance, the universe wrapping around itself so that each of its smallest particles contained the whole universe. Each tree could contain the whole forest, each branch of the tree the whole tree, and each cell of the branch the whole branch. We may see that this type of circularity still evokes a sense of infinity; if in reaching the smallest part we encounter once again the whole, we will never find a resting point or a point of finality to our picture.

Infinity and circularity are the basic characteristics of our picture of the world insofar as we regard it as being devoid of atoms. If we do regard it as containing atoms, then the atoms itself will take on the mystical quality, in that an atom is something which can never be described or thought about. What is the meaning of the "A" in "A is A?" Most people would regard this as a meaningless question.

These reflections uncover a basic limitation to our knowledge of the world. If the world has atoms, then we cannot know anything about those atoms. If the world does not have atoms but does have relations, then either the world will be infinite and thus never fully knowable, or it will be described circularly and thus all of our knowledge of it will be circular. If the world has neither atoms nor relations, then there is nothing that can be known about the world.

There is a way in which we may eliminate the need for atoms in *Chapter Ten's* notation: this is by replacing atoms with relations relating themselves to themselves. To do this will shed light on the concept of an atom, and show that really it is in a sense inconceivable.

A relation, in the notation of *Chapter Ten*, consists of taking two units, joining them by an arrow, and drawing a circle around the whole construction. We may then obviate the need for atoms by, wherever we would use an atom, instead using a relation where each of the units joined by the arrow is the circle drawn around the whole construction. This can be drawn like Fig 18:

Fig. 18: Atom Relation

It can also be drawn as in Fig 19, with the disadvantage that this figure violates the rule of the arrow remaining within the circle:

Fig. 19: Alternative Atom Relation 1

Alternatively, we may allow the arrow to fall into congruence with the circle as in Fig 20:

Fig. 20: Alternative Atom Relation 2

In this case the notation converges upon the empty circle, and we may understand the empty circles in the figures in this way if we wish to say that our notation does not employ atoms.

Such a figure may be understood as representing a duality, or as representing a unity — it is thus a paradoxical equivocation of the two. It is precisely the paradox of an all-encompassing unity that it must also encompass duality, and this is here captured pictorially.

As the basic unit of existence, the atom is beyond being this way or that way, but rather is everything and nothing. It would have to be so, because everything springs forth from it, and therefore nothing can contain anything that was not contained in the atom from the beginning. The inherently paradoxical and non-logical nature of the atom is captured in its re-conception as the relation relating itself to itself. The relation is love, and the relation relating itself to itself is love's self-recognition and love of itself for itself.

It is my suspicion that there is no single picture of the world. Rather, I suspect that we could draw numerous different pictures of the world, having a great diversity in their construction, and that each such picture would leave something out. With each such picture we could modify it to incorporate some particular thing that was left out, but there would always be something else that still went unmentioned. This point of view is supported by such results as Gödel's incompleteness theorem.

We have been accustomed in this treatise to understanding the world as a multiplicity of mathematical pattern. Gödel's incompleteness theorem, which we discussed earlier, suggests that the totality of possible mathematical pattern, being infinite, cannot be summarized in any finite form. There is no set of axioms from which we could derive all mathematical truths. Now, if we take the world as the totality of mathematical pattern, this will mean for us that the world is infinite, and that it will therefore always surpass our knowledge of it.

The conclusion is that no picture can be made of the world; we can only picture parts of the world. This is the case if the world is infinite. It is impossible to draw a picture of something that is infinite, though it is possible to draw a picture of a part of something that is infinite. Infinity has no boundaries, and so there would be no place to draw the boundaries of the picture. Infinity has infinitely many component parts, which is a different way of saying that it has no component parts. Thus when one pictures infinity, one has no picture.

If we regard the world as infinite, this requires us to abandon a particular concept of the world. Science and common sense agree in providing us with this concept of the world, which states: the world is made of objects, which are themselves concatenations of smaller objects. The world itself is simply the largest object, and is the concatenation of all of the objects.

Let us illustrate this concept. A city contains many blocks. A block contains many buildings. A building contains many rooms. One of these rooms contains me. I contain many organs. These organs contain many cells. These cells contain many molecules. These molecules contain many atoms.

According to science and common sense, we continue enumerating the objects in the world in this way and eventually arrive at a total picture of the world. In other words, we conceive of the world as the sum of the various things it contains, and therefore itself a thing made up of many other things. If the world is infinite, then the world is not the sum of the things inside it, and furthermore the world itself is not a thing. Nor can we say what it is, in that no complete description of it is possible.

"Thou hast no right but to do thy will."

- Aleister Crowley, The Book of the Law

12

SOLILOQUY ON FREE WILL AND THE WORLD

PART THREE

A **PHILOSOPHY** is a part of the universe which attempts to represent the universe: to recapitulate the meaning of the totality in a piece thereof. Philosophy accomplishes this goal by finding, through the search of all of the different patterns that present themselves in the universe, those patterns which resonate with the greatest clarity with the whole.

Philosophy does not begin from nothing, because first of all in order to begin to philosophize one must already have a universe in existence. Furthermore, the extraction of pattern from this universe does not begin with nothing; rather, it begins with the patterns that have been extracted by the mind of the individual in the totality of their life experience; and these patterns have themselves been built upon that extracted pattern which has been built up by the human race since its inception.

The test of the value of a philosophy is the clarity and volume of its resonance with the totality of life experience. This test of resonance is not applied directly to the whole of the universe, but is instead applied to the representation of the universe which has been built up in the memory of the individual. Thus the individual who contemplates philosophy is in fact *the medium in which philosophy operates*, and the philosophy is to be validated by the effect which it produces in this medium. The ability to create a powerful movement in consciousness indicates the philosophy's resonance with the universe as a whole as represented in the memory of the individual.

This naïve notion of the equivalence of truth and meaning is represented in the instinctive approach to philosophy which is taken by anybody who is not acquainted with the approach of rationality. This approach, rationality, has been developed gradually over the centuries within the tradition of Western thought, and it places emphasis not on the inner response of the individual to an idea, but on the fine-tuning of symbolic representation of ideas according to the carrying out of mechanical methods of validation and invalidation: the proof in mathematics, the experiment in science, the argument in philosophy.

These methods operate as heuristic techniques for extracting from the search space those ideas likely to have the highest degree of resonance within the domain in question. Mathematics and science have benefited enormously from their use. Philosophy has largely suffered, and the success of its peers in using these same methods has blinded it to this fact. The reason for the lack of success of rationality in philosophy is that philosophy's domain of inquiry is not a particular area of existence such as imaginary numbers or North American birds or digestive enzymes, but the totality of life experience as represented in the totality of the mind of the inquirer themselves. In philosophy the problem is not one of fine-tuning a solution that is basically correct, but of finding solutions of progressively increasing quality with no obtainable upper limit to this quality, or many significant restricting parameters to the forms that the solutions may take. We must proceed without the expectation that any of these solutions will prove a final and satisfactory explanation of life experience, which is so large a topic of inquiry that our highest ambition can be to gain glimpses of its meaning. Because the nature of the problem in philosophy is utterly different from the nature of the problems in math and science, the methods that have worked so well for math and science fail miserably for philosophy. Not only in philosophy can we not hope for a tidy solution of our domain of inquiry, but we cannot hope either for a tidy solution to the problem of how to go about the inquiring.

I arrived at the formalism presented in the previous chapter not through a process of stepwise, rational development, but by an unsystematic process of exploring the solution space of possible modes of symbolizing reality. It has been my experience that the mode of symbolic representation of reality holds some significance, in that a symbolism more resonant with the various orders of pattern in reality will offer a more efficacious tool for the structuring and manipulation of intuition in such a way as to yield the experience of meaning. It is probable that this particular tool is tooled not only to orders of pattern in reality, but to orders of pattern in my own mind, such that it would be of greatest use to one whose mind was structured similarly to my own. Therefore I present it in the hope that it proves helpful to somebody but without the pretense of attempting to convince anybody of its significance.

The notion of unity and duality deserves further elaboration; there are numerous perspectives from which it may be studied and understood. My ability to carry out this elaboration is unfortunately limited by my own relative paucity of understanding of the notion. It has been a subject of my continuous contemplation for about a year now, but I do not have the feeling that I grasp its meaning at all, though I apprehend it more vividly than any other idea.

The positive may be understood as self, and the negative as other. "Self" is to be conceived as a singular and unified sphere of consciousness, and may be envisioned as light. "Other" is that which is unseen and hidden from consciousness, and thus constitutes an inconceivably vast expanse which may be envisioned as darkness. Between these two lies the event horizon of experience.

Recall that the universe may be pictured as an elaborate, static arrangement of dyads. Under this point of view every unit may be taken as a self, opposed to the "otherness" of everything else existing, and one may then pose the question of how the universe subjectively appears from the point of view of any of its parts. One thus obtains the "sphere whose center is everywhere and whose circumference is nowhere found" spoken of in various occult contexts.

The event horizon of experience, the meeting place of light and darkness, is phenomenal existence itself. Light and darkness are in themselves both unknown *unknowables*; darkness invisible because it is by definition that which is never illuminated, and light invisible because it is that which does the illuminating. (One cannot see light; one can only see objects off of which light reflects.) That which is experienced, therefore, is neither light nor darkness, but that which is revealed in their coming together.

If one illuminates a darkened place, the various things contained in it will become visible. This is the pattern which we see in all discovery; mathematics illuminates the world of mathematical pattern, linguistics the world of linguistic pattern, the microscope the world of microscopic pattern, etc. We are not inventing things as we discover them; rather, they were there all along, simply waiting for us to illuminate them and render them visible.

Similarly, we may understand that all of the future possibilities of the world are not a giant question mark, but rather may be hypothesized by inference from the present, and subsequently discovered. If a person, finding themselves in a new situation, makes a new choice which they have not made before, the possibility and probability of their making that choice could have been seen to a greater or lesser extent beforehand. The present is made of pieces of the past, and a person's past history delineates their future possibilities. The choosing thus acts as a light which shines upon a person's past, in that every choice a person makes shows in more and more detail the constitution of their being, which is to say their history. The movement into the future is thus the uncovering of the past. Every new event or experiment merely adds to our knowledge of history.

It is thus by analyzing and understanding our past that we are able to decide our futures wisely. A person does not enter every situation as if it were the first time they were in that situation; rather, the weight of the past steers them. Only by thoroughly understanding their past is a person able to shape their future. History, and especially self-history, is however a very difficult discipline, because we must be able to distinguish the past as it is from the past as we have been told it is, and the past as it is from the past as we wish it was. It is difficult for us to know the truth about ourselves because it so often happens that the truth is not what we thought or hoped it to be. A person cannot go on forever in faith that they are otherwise than they are; it must eventually happen we are brought face to face with who we in fact are, and compelled to accept this reality of ourselves.

Such self-discovery is a basic outcome of all of our activities, and through it we assemble a picture of ourselves and the world in which we live. One of the basic questions we ought to answer about ourselves is: "what are we after?" If a person knows certainly and without error what they are after, it is impossible for them to act randomly and thus waste their time, or to vacillate between one set of motives and another thus repeatedly undoing their own work. That we in fact do both of these things indicates that we do not know what we are after. I will make some observations in an attempt to shed light on this problem.

SOLILOQUY ON FREE WILL AND THE WORLD
PART THREE

The phenomenon of hierarchical clustering presented in *Chapter Ten* is not merely a geographical, static phenomenon; rather, it is an organismic phenomenon of *growth*, unfolding over time and moving towards greater units of clustering as time progresses. From this observation we see that the basic movement of existence is from small and simple existences to large and complex existences, in a process of small existences joining with each other. This we may see straightforwardly in the natural world, where each unit of life attempts to build itself into ever more life, and also in social existence, where precisely the same phenomenon occurs with political, ideological, and religious movements (moving towards greater power), with love-relationships (moving towards greater love), with areas of knowledge (moving towards greater clarity of vision), and so on.

Those who thought that the universe could be understood as a balanced interplay of creative and destructive forces, in which neither creation nor destruction wins out positively, misapprehended the universe. In human spheres, what appears to be wanton destruction is almost always in reality an attempt to empower another entity other than the one being destroyed; and two forces in conflict, mutually tearing at each other, are each vying for their own growth. The only truly destructive forces are blind, random physical catastrophes — viz., a hurricane or a volcano[1]. These forces are rather the exception than the rule — physical phenomena being the least developed type of phenomenon.

The tyranny of the physical sciences over modern thought has brought us under the illusion that the rules that apply in the world of dead matter are those dictating existence in general; but it is clear to any straightforward observation that dead matter is the least powerful, the least evolved aspect of existence. In the sphere of life the rule is not a standing wave of creation and destruction; rather, it is a continual movement towards life, ever more life. Life is not destructive; it is creative through and through; it only ever destroys to prepare for a still greater creation.

This creation is through assimilation, through binding-together, or to use a loaded term through "love." An organism seeks out nutrition and light, attempting to increase the matter and energy which constitutes itself. A person seeks out love, knowledge, relationships,

---

[1] Although, even these 'blind' destructive forces pave the way for new creative opportunities.

positions, hoping to give itself up to larger units of life and to bring more life under its power. *Will* is precisely the will to life, and *love under will* is thus the process in which life is continually engaged. This process, beginning with dead matter, yields organic life, and organic life yields self-conscious, intelligent life, which builds for itself social structures of progressively increasing complexity. One may contemplate the breathtaking vistas of possibility implicit in the future of this grand process of "love under will."

Let us then examine this "will." I mean the word in quite a simple sense; that is, it refers to ambition, desire, lust, motivation — all of the energy keeping our psychological life in motion. This is what the word means initially. But I also mean it in a more general sense, and the question arises of how far outwards the meaning of the word extends.

We are to understand emotions — joy, sorrow, etc. — as manifestations of the will. They are after all "e-motions," which is to say motions of psyche, and will is that driving energy responsible for all psychological motion. Now is it clear that joy and sorrow are willed — or on the other hand, can we conceive of them as passive affects, imposed upon the psyche rather than created by the psyche?

The perplexity in this case is created by a reversal of the roles of will and its object. In the case of ambition and related affects, will is the mover, and the object the moved; while in the case of emotions, the object is the mover, and will the moved. In an emotion, our psyche is affected or overcome by something outside ourselves, and in this sense emotion is a passive mode. But without will this being affected should be impossible, for it is precisely the friction on the one hand between will and outside force, and the resonance on the other hand between the two, that constitutes the inner structure of the emotion. In emotion, the will plays the role of victim rather than perpetrator, but we should not therefore conclude that emotion is pure passivity; for without the will's affirmation or denial this passivity should be one of indifferently being moved, after the manner of dead matter.

In contrast to the passive mode of emotions, thought may be construed as an active mode of the will, in which the will manipulates and correlates the contents of memory towards one end or another. This is most obvious in directed thinking, where the singularity of purpose is clear; where that which may be called "mind-wandering" appears more as a constant fluctuation of the will, where everything willed is willed so briefly that it hardly seems as if it were an act of will at all.

Joy and sorrow are the nature of our relations to the forces that are greater than us, and thus are the basic forms of the *religious* will. Unless we are to conceive of ourselves in the role of the creator, the prophet, or the magician, our relations with existence at large will be passive relations of being affected, and thus in the nature of sorrow and joy. And because in these relations our will becomes the point of discharge of the greater will of existence at large, these experiences of joy and sorrow will be the most profound ones available to us.

I have tacitly made the assumption that *a larger will exists*, in gross contradiction to the modern assumption, reinforced by the investigations of science, that the only wills are our individual human wills. I wish to defend this conclusion, but before I do so I will find it necessary to defend the more general conclusion of the existence of a larger-than-human *consciousness*, for consciousness would seem to be the necessary precondition to will, from which we may imagine will proceeding almost without intermediate steps.[2]

First we ought to ask another preliminary question: can we conceive of consciousness without will? This would seem to be a matter of intuition, but my own answer is, "yes." This consciousness would merely be a shadowy, unmoving sphere of silent awareness, in which little or no activity took place. We may think of dreamless sleep or of the infant in the womb. Then again, some might call these states precisely states of un-consciousness!

In investigating the question of larger-than-human consciousness, it is wise to begin by delineating carefully the widely accepted modern position on this question, as suggested by the results of science.

In this position, human consciousness is the only consciousness that we posit to exist, for the reason that it is the only consciousness for which we can see any evidence. Furthermore, this consciousness is an epiphenomenon of the human nervous system; that is to say, there is nothing to consciousness that does not belong to the nervous

---

2 Will is, after all, the first manifestation of consciousness. Before an organism thinks, feels, or perceives, it wills. Consider a bacterium, which is unable to carry out any cognitive process, but is nonetheless able to struggle for its survival. In the primordial emergence of the mind, whatever we choose to label as the first organism to have a mind, it is surely the case that thinking, feeling, and sensing were late-comers compared to willing. Consider also the infant, whose first indications of possessing consciousness are always those of wanting or denying.

system, no "soul" or "spirit" or "mind-stuff," and if we posit a "mind" at all, in doing so we are only speaking of the nervous system from a psychological perspective and in psychological language. Under this perspective, every statement about the human mind may therefore be translated into a statement about the physical states of neurons, proteins, electrical signals, and so forth. Even a statement such as "I am conscious" should then find a translation into purely physiological terms, leading some researchers to attempt to locate the cortical region or neurotransmitter responsible for consciousness.

What are the factors that have led to this perspective? We may name several briefly. There is the scientific approach of studying the world through sensory perceptions (what it calls the "objective") rather than through internal perceptions (what it calls the "subjective"), which is related to the difficulty in coming to any kind of consensus on propositions concerning these latter perceptions. It is also related to the great success of disciplines such as physics, chemistry, and biology in describing the patterns which our sensory perceptions assume. The grand assumption is then made that "the world" is equal to "the world described by various mathematical models developed from analysis of our sensory perceptions," with the only major potential criticism of this assumption being the possibility that the world of which our internal perceptions are the horizon is not congruent with the world of which our sensory perceptions are the horizon,[3] since after all only the latter perceptions enter into the studies which have led to the models of the physical sciences, and it might turn out that the internal perceptions were not explainable in terms of the models developed to explain the sensory perceptions. The assumption that the two *are* congruent, however, is powerfully validated by recent developments in the field of neuroscience which have made it possible to explain many (and the suspicion is, all), psychological phenomena in terms of the models developed by the physical sciences.

The phenomenon of consciousness is one of these internal

---

[3] The perspective we are discussing suggests that our sensory perceptions are the beginning of a vast expanse of further similar existence, which has appeared progressively vaster the more it has been studied, while on the other hand that our internal perceptions do not imply such a vast expanse, but only a small, personal world. It is interesting to ask whether this might be due to a bias in the methods of study, or whether there is some more convincing reason for this asymmetry.

perceptions, or perhaps the central such perception. Now if it turned out that internal perceptions were *not* explainable in the vocabulary of the physical sciences, the question of whether or not there exists larger-than-human consciousness would then be a question to be answered without reference to the physical sciences, and the fact that science shows us no such thing would have no bearing on the question of whether or not it existed. The question would then seem to be an open one — or rather, we would be offered all of the answers given by the philosophers, psychologists, and religions down through the ages, and it would not be clear that any of these stood on solid ground.

Let us then make the opposite assumption, that internal perceptions are explainable in the vocabulary of the physical sciences, and consciousness is a purely physical phenomenon. What should we then conclude about the question of whether or not there exists larger-than-human consciousness?

Let us begin by reiterating the usual position, but now in the language of the physical sciences. There is an unimaginably vast expanse of space and matter. On one such concentration of matter (the Earth) there is an imperceptibly small film of material called "organic life." Some pieces of this matter called "nervous systems" have the property "conscious." In all the universe only such pieces of matter have this property.

Now, a nervous system is a mass of protein and fat arranged in an exquisitely complicated pattern. The exquisitely complicated pattern is essential to producing the property "conscious," and even miniscule changes in the pattern can cause this property to go away. It is therefore obvious that any arbitrary mass of protein and fat does not have this property. Furthermore, any arbitrary mass of matter which is not protein and fat does not have this property. Thus we see that it is only in inconceivably specific configurations of matter that this property "conscious" arises.

Now, are we to regard the property "conscious" as basically different in nature from other physical properties? Consider the difference between sawing a person's arm off (without anesthesia or their consent) and sawing a piece of plywood (again with neither of these things). The only reason we regard these events as different is because of the property "conscious" possessed by the nervous system connected with the arm, and we see from this example what a large difference this property seems to us to make.

But it is necessary to apprehend consciousness independent of any of its particular modes (such as pain in the previous example), and to consider consciousness as it is at all times, rather than as it is at some times. When one strips away all of its temporary affects, there is indeed a sense of consciousness as it is in general, which however is at most times hidden by the particular forms which consciousness assumes. Then, according to the perspective we are considering, we are this, and a piece of iron is not. Now, either we assert that ourselves and the iron are *not* different in this regard, or if we believe that we are different then we are left with the extraordinary task of explaining *how*. From the perspective of the physical sciences, the differences are almost nil; it is, as previously noted, inconceivably minute and intricate changes in physical state which make the difference between "conscious" and "not conscious." We are therefore required to believe that these inconceivably minute and intricate changes in physical state create this vast and inexplicable difference in the nature of the phenomenon. At least, that is what we are required to believe if we wish to make the assumption that this property "conscious" is only possessed by nervous systems.

At this point it may be re-emphasized that the idea that only nervous systems are conscious is indeed an assumption of assumptions, in that there is no evidence in the entire scientific corpus to indicate that it might be the case. Our evidence that *we are conscious* is subjective but undeniable; and our evidence that *any given thing other than ourselves is or is not conscious* would seem to be in every case nonexistent, because we have for no such thing evidence of consciousness like the evidence we have for our own consciousness. We can argue that Occam's razor should lead us to refrain from positing the consciousness of anything other than ourselves; but first of all, on this line of thinking Occam's razor would actually recommend solipsism, which is not what we had in mind; and secondly, in view of the foregoing considerations it seems that in reality the theory that nervous systems are the only thing that are conscious is *anything but* the simplest theory! On the contrary, to justify it, when it is considered in detail, would seem to require the most exquisite contortions of thinking.

At the root of this assumption, I argue, is a certain bias towards the conception of consciousness as anthropomorphic. That is, when we imagine "being conscious," we can only imagine "being humanly conscious," but there may be other modes of being conscious more or less unfamiliar to us. To answer the question "is there non-human consciousness?" by invoking the possibility of aliens is to retain the bias towards the anthropomorphization of consciousness. We are required to imagine a consciousness whose properties are basically different; e.g., a piece of iron could be conscious after its own fashion without therefore being able to think or to feel pain.

Anthropomorphic biases have colored our thought at all times. Thus in animistic world-views, all things are conceived of as conscious, and specifically conceived of as anthropomorphically conscious. In the field of religion, God has usually been supposed to be anthropomorphically conscious, and though more sophisticated theological perspectives would regard this as an absurdity, the intuition persists. It is perhaps only with the advent of science that a thoroughgoing conception of a non-anthropomorphic world has dawned upon humanity. It is possible that we made a fundamental error in formulating this world-view[4] when, having seen the obvious fact that a star or an electron would not be anthropomorphically conscious, we then concluded that these entities would be *unconscious*, and thus unwittingly arrived at the bizarre perspective outlined previously. It is perhaps the simpler view to imagine vast vistas of consciousness quite different from our human consciousness.

Let us briefly review. Our experience seems to us to be divided into two regions — the sensory or "objective," and the internal mental/emotional, or "subjective." Science studies only the "objective" aspect of our experience, and makes the assumption that the "subjective" aspect can be explained in terms of the models developed to explain the "objective." We considered two possibilities. Firstly, if this assumption is false, then the question of whether or not there is larger-than-human consciousness would seem to be an open one. Secondly, if this assumption is true, it would seem to be simplest to suppose that there is larger-than-human consciousness, as the physical world is much larger than humans, and there are great conceptual difficulties involved in maintaining that nervous systems are the only type of matter which is conscious when this claim is examined in detail.

These are the grounds on which we place the notion of larger-than-human consciousness. What, then, of larger-than-human *will*? For instance, is the physical world a representation of the will of some

---

4 The world-view suggested by science must be understood as distinct from the formal results of science.

cosmic being? Here we return to the question of the types of forces existing. In the co-created restricted, deterministic, or deterministic stochastic theory, as these theories are described in *Chapter Ten*, there will exist forces determining the manner of being of the universe which are not wills. In these theories, physical laws will not be the will of a cosmic being. In the co-created theory, the physical laws must represent such a will, because there is nothing else which they could represent.

What determines the universe? Is the universe an impersonal machine into which we are thrust? Or, is the universe something that the totality of free will created for itself? If the latter, what is the totality of free will, and how do we stand in relationship to it?

The notion of "force" is basic to science, and indeed so basic that its nature is hardly ever questioned or made a topic of inquiry. In concerning itself with determining the details of the manner of force's operation, science has neglected the question, "what is force?" The implicit supposition is that force is an unconscious, dead, mechanical process. But we can imagine force also as *living force*, as the force of free will, and in this case we will have to imagine the universe not as existing as the chance mechanical output of a universe-generating machine, but as existing out of a will to exist.

The understanding of force as a mechanical process runs into a basic limit point, where it stops and goes no further. This we can see by examination of a certain mathematical paradox, whose explanation will require the exposition of some intervening material.

It was shown by Alan Turing and Alonzo Church that all mechanical processes above a certain level of complexity are equivalent to each other. There is a certain class of mechanical processes called "Turing-equivalent," which class includes all computers, and certain mathematical and logical formalisms. Any Turing-equivalent machine can carry out any process that any other Turing-equivalent machine can carry out. This means that, for instance, a program written for any computer can in principle be re-written for any other computer. It also means that within any Turing-equivalent machine, one can build a simulation of any other Turing-equivalent machine.

The first surprising fact we see here, then, is that all of these different systems converge on a common set of capabilities once they reach a certain level of capability. The second surprising fact we can observe is that it appears to be physically impossible, and perhaps even logically impossible, to construct a computer which is more than Turing-equivalent: that is, a computer which could carry out any process that a Turing-equivalent machine could not carry out. What this suggests is that in Turing-equivalence we have uncovered not simply a limitation of computers, but a limitation of the world.

Now, suppose that we adopt the hypothesis that the world is a Turing-equivalent machine. This would be the case if and only if it were possible to construct a computer simulation of the world. (We here ignore the fact that such a simulation would require a computer larger than the universe.) If we take science and mathematics as true descriptions of the workings of the world, then we are led to such a point of view, since it is probably the case that all of the rules posited by science and mathematics can be quantified and written into a computer program, insofar as those rules are themselves coherent and internally consistent.

If we adopt the hypothesis that the world is a Turing-equivalent machine, we are confronted with the following paradox: *what is running the machine?* A Turing-equivalent machine requires as substrate another machine which is also Turing-equivalent. It is common in computer technology practice to have several nested levels of Turing-equivalent systems, and the first of these levels will be the hardware whose substrate is our physical reality. If we are working under the supposition that this physical reality is itself a Turing-equivalent machine, we will create the same requirement for it: that is, we will pose the question of the substrate on which our physical reality rests. Now, either we posit an infinite series of Turing-equivalent machines (if that would be enough!), or we are forced to imagine a machine that runs itself (a most mind-bending paradox), or we are forced to posit that if our physical reality is mechanical, it rests upon a foundation which is itself non-mechanical. There will be a "ghost in the machine," which itself could not be quantified or studied in a systematic manner.

"Things cannot go beyond the extreme. When they reach their limit, they turn back to their origin."

- Gua 24, I Ching

13

TURNING BACK

WE are coming to the end of our brief glance at rationality and mysticism. Writing a book such as this is a frustrating process, because the nature of the subject matter is such that one can never exhaust it or even treat it adequately. At so many junctures one feels entirely without words. One can never explain the perfected orderliness and fastidious weaving together of all facts which is the essence of rationality; nor can one explain the ecstatic melting of all into unity which is the essence of mysticism. So a book such as this will always be a disappointment in relation to the goal which it sets for itself.

Before we end it is worth stepping back and taking a broad view on what we have accomplished. We explained that mysticism consists of three things: mystical experience, mystical practices, and mystical thinking. Mystical practices are things done to induce mystical experiences; and mystical thinking is the attempt to articulate the truths which mystical experience seems to reveal.

Mystical thinking includes two important divisions: metaphysics, and archetypal thinking. Metaphysics is a logical discipline which speculates about the nature of reality, basing its conclusions on intuitions. Archetypal thinking is an experiential discipline which studies the abstract roots of human experience - i.e., the "archetypes."

We then saw that mystical thinking is opposed to rationality. Rationality is the way of seeking truth which is practiced in science and mathematics. The two are in conflict because the beliefs, and the ways of determining beliefs, involved in mystical thinking are unacceptable to rationality. Rationality tells us that we should determine our beliefs through reasoning and evidence;

while mystical thinking determines its beliefs through intuition and experience.

A serious conflict between rationality and mysticism has to do with materialism. Rationality tells us that materialism is true. But materialism is inconsistent with mysticism because it tells us that we live in an amoral, ethically indifferent world in which there is no guarantee of a brighter future and no guarantee that we will become enlightened.

Most of us desire to synthesize rationality and mysticism. Rationality is a sound way of seeking the truth which can help us to think more clearly and determine our beliefs in a rigorous and bulletproof way. Mysticism is a way of seeking the truth which can shed light on things that rationality cannot comprehend. Mysticism can transform our experience and help us to lead better lives. Since both of these disciplines have much to offer us, it is worth our time to attempt to work out the conflict between them.

We can solve part of the conflict by invoking the distinction between logic and experience. These are two archetypes. Logic is the mental faculty of calculating, drawing relations, and making deductions. Experience is every aspect of human consciousness which is not logic. Rationality is entirely a logical discipline; and mysticism is mostly an experiential discipline. Simply pointing out this fact solves much of the conflict between them. Things which are in the domain of experience cannot be in conflict with rationality, because they have nothing to do with it. Many of the puzzling statements of the mystics actually have no logical meaning, and by virtue of that fact they cannot be irrational.

Some conflict between rationality and mysticism remains after pointing this out. This conflict has to do with metaphysics and materialism. Metaphysics is the logical aspect of mysticism. It involves beliefs which violate the epistemology of rationality, and which are inconsistent with rational beliefs such as materialism.

One solution to this problem is to reject metaphysics. This solution runs into a serious difficulty, however, with the aforementioned existential problems with materialism. It seems that some metaphysical beliefs are necessary in order to make mysticism tenable as a worldview and way of living. We need a *guarantee* of the possibility of enlightenment, which seems to necessitate life after death. We also require that the universe be constructed such that it is ethical.

So we cannot reject metaphysics; we need to find a different way to solve its conflict with rationality. We can do this by revising the rationality epistemology. The rationalist epistemology states that we should determine our beliefs based on reasoning and evidence. We say, instead, that we should determine beliefs based on reasoning, evidence, and intuitions. We say that our intuitions are a source of knowledge, and that we can know things about the world directly through these intuitions. This provides the basis which we need to establish metaphysics. It not only solves the problems of metaphysics and materialism, but also opens up countless new lines of interesting research in which we attempt to determine truths about reality through our intuitions.

We concluded our synthesis of rationality and mysticism with a discussion of what rationality tells us about how to engage in mystical practice. It tells us to determine through experiment what works and does not work, without reliance on authority. Taking this approach reveals that there is nothing simple and easy to describe which makes a significant difference in mystical practice.

Next we departed from the rationality/mysticism problem and considered mysticism by itself. We said that all human despair can be thought of as facing nothingness; and then we turned this concept on it head by equating nothingness with the mystical, expressing the concept of transforming sorrow into joy.

Continuing our contemplation of the relationship between mysticism and the emotional life, we explored the duality of joy and sorrow, turning these two about in their various relationships to each other, and seeking the concept of their non-duality.

Finally, we attempted to construct a metaphysical conception of the universe which thought of all existent things as emerging from a primal duality, which duality emerged from, and is one with, a primal unity.

A disappointing thing about these inquiries was that none of them could really pin down the essence of mystical truth that lies behind every distortion. This, of course, was due to the very nature of that truth; and we knew at the beginning that things would turn out this way. This is why the genuine inquiry into truth finds itself always at the beginning, and with every step forward it takes, it finds itself still at the beginning. Begin!

INDEX

Advaita vedanta 138, 152
Anthropomorphism 193
Archetypes 71, 73, 81, 116
  and non-archetypes 81
  archetypal thinking 72, 73, 87
    compatibility with rationality 86
    Plato, Theory of Forms 73
    relationship to metaphysics 87
  characteristics
    abstraction 73
    experienceability 73
    human universality 73
    pervasiveness 73
    resistance to logical analysis 73
  knowledge of 81, 84
    archetypal significations 81
    individual archetypes 81
    relations between archetypes 82
  relations 82
    inclusion 83
    opposition 82
    similarity 82
  systems of archetypes 73, 85

Bible 125, 151
Blavatsky, Helena 109

Charitability, principle of 91, 106
Comedy and tragedy 151
Consciousness 5–7, 19–23, 31, 88, 97, 106, 109, 143, 150, 155, 162, 176, 183, 185, 189–193, 198
  phenomenon of 190

Despair 129, 133
  and ephemerality 131
  and eternal pain 133
  and knowledge, passion of 131
  and love and hate 130
  and nothing matters 133
  and transience of the self 132
  from unhappy circumstances 129
  and pain 134
  solution to 134

Despair *cont'd*
  the ladder of 130
  where I am nothing 135–136
  where nothing is real 135
Dhammapada 102
  Analysis of 103
Dyads. *See* Symbolism, dyads

Ecstasy 150–151, 155
Emerald tablet 112
  analysis of 112
Emotions 19, 27, 28, 32, 96, 97, 148, 188
Epistemology 59, 68, 69
Experience 68, 185, 193, 198
  and self discovery 186–187
  as archetypes 81

Gödel, Kurt 58, 172, 180

Happiness and sorrow 143–155
Heart sutra 104

Immutable laws 162–164, 166
Intuitions 60, 68, 69
Isis unveiled, Helena Blavatsky 109
  analysis of 110

Katha upanishad 94
  analysis of 95

Leibniz 177
Logic 28
  and Metaphysics 62
  conflicts of 61
  logic and experience 28–30
  Russell, Bertrand 28
Love 34, 73, 83, 84, 130, 131, 133, 144, 149, 151, 155, 173

Materialism 61, 63, 65, 66, 198
  and death 65
  and the Universe 66

INDEX

Materialism *cont'd*
  conflict with mysticism 64, 66
  materialists 68
  rejection of 66, 68, 69
Mathematics 52, 173, 175, 184, 190
  and structure of reality 175
  patterns 180–181
  set theory 83, 174
Metamathematics 58
Metaphysics 61, 87, 197, 198
  as theoretical mystical thinking 72
  fake justifications of 62
  relationship with archetypal thinking 87
Mundaka upanishad 92
  analysis of 93
Mystical experience 67, 121, 197
  and expectations of 121
  definition 19
  emotional aspects 20
  examples of 19–25
  explanation of 19
  insights 20
  of the mystical 83
  psychological perspective 19
  religious perspective 19
  sensory phenomena 20
  synonyms 19
Mystical philosophy 158
Mystical practices 119, 197
  and concentration 123–124
  and irrationality 120
  important conditions for 120
  in relation to rationality 119
  lesser banishing ritual of pentagram 122
  living in the mystical 125
  using one's own intelligence 122
Mystical thinking 16
Mystical thinking 71, 116, 197
  and archetypes 71
  and rationality 72
  types of
    practical 72
    theoretical 72
      archetypal thinking 72
      metaphysics 72
Mysticism 16, 64, 125, 157, 198
  and life after death 65
  and optimism 65, 67
  conflict with materialism 64
  Jewish 138
  living in 125
  mystical ideas 34
  mystics, justification of 68

Mysticism *cont'd*
  non-mystics, justification of 68

Nietzsche 149
Non-dualism. *See* Philosophy, non-dualism
Nothingness 129–141, 154–155
  and something 141
Oahspe 107
  analysis of 108
Organic life 169

Pain
  as pleasure 149
Passion 150–151, 155
Philosophy 158, 183
  difficulty of explaining mystical concepts 71
  dualism 82, 95, 98, 99, 101, 102, 109, 113, 114, 115, 127, 152, 157–160, 158, 161, 176, 180, 185, 199
  monism 157–160
  mystical 158
  non-dualism 83, 148, 152–153
  unity 23, 24, 109, 110, 128, 144, 146, 147, 151, 154, 157, 173, 176, 180, 185, 197, 199
  value of 183
  western 27
    empiria (experience) 27
    logos (reason) 27

Randomness 169
  true randomness 161, 162–164, 166
  vs. free will 162
Rationality 37–55, 57, 59, 88, 184, 197, 198
  and belief 45
  and conflict of mystical thinking 72
  and evidence 52
  and justification 45
  and resolving disagreements 53
  and skepticism 48
  and trust 50
  and truth 37–45
  compatibility with archetypal thinking 86
  definition of 37
  in philosophy 184
Rationality and mysticism
  reconciliation of 32–35
Reason and experience
  distinction 27–28

INDEX

Reason and experience *cont'd*
  explanation 27–28
Reductionism 30–32, 64
Reincarnation 65
Russell, Bertrand 28

Samadhi 147
Sorrow 143
States of affairs 161–162, 166
  co-created 164, 165, 194
  co-created restricted 164, 165, 194
  co-created restricted stochastic 164
  co-created stochastic 164
  deterministic 164, 165, 194
  deterministic stochastic 164
  random 164
Symbolism 166, 167, 169, 171, 184
  atoms 177, 178, 181
  binary code 166
  clusters 168, 169, 171
  dyads 175, 185
  heterogeneous cluster 169
  hierarchical clustering 167, 187
    and growth 187
  Mandelbrot set 177
  representation of ideas 184
  representing the universe 171

Tao Te Ching 125, 139
  chapter 2 98
    analysis of 98
  chapter 77 100
    analysis of 101
Thelema 138, 139, 152–154
  hadit 152
  nuit 152
  the book of the law 138, 153
Tragedy 144, 151
Truth 199
Turing, Alan 194
  and Church, Alonzo 194
  Turing-equivalent machine 194–195

Universe 65, 194
  and balance 187
  and materialism 66
  and ultimate Goodness 67
  experiential 68
  laws of physics 66
Upanishad
  Katha 94
  Mundaka 92

Will 160–164, 188
  free will 162–166, 194
  vs. true randomness 162–163

www.ingramcontent.com/pod-product-compliance
Lightning Source LLC
LaVergne TN
LVHW041542070426
835507LV00011B/874